Gypsy Witch Presents: Tropical Spells Hoodoos & Voodoos

Includes the Rare Manuscript
THE BLACK PULLET

Edited By Dragonstar

INNER LIGHT PUBLICATIONS

GYPSY WITCH PRESENTS:
TROPICAL SPELLS HOODOOS & VOODOOS

GYPSY WITCH PRESENTS:
TROPICAL SPELLS HOODOOS & VOODOOS

Edited by Dragonstar

Copyright © 2010 - Inner Light Publications, All Rights Reserved

ISBN-10: 1-60611-075-6
ISBN-13: 978-1-60611-075-1

Nonfiction – Metaphysics

No part of this book may be reproduced, stored in retrieval system or transmitted in any form or by any means, electronic, mechanical, photocopying, recording, without express permission of the publisher.

Timothy Green Beckley: Editorial Director
Carol Rodriguez: Publishers Assistant
Tim Swartz: Associate Editor
Sean Casteel: Editorial Assistant
William Kern: Editorial Assistant
Cover Art: Tim Swartz

1. Beckley, Timothy, Dragonstar, Magical Arts, Metaphysics, History – Nonfiction

I. Title: **Gypsy Witch Presents: Tropical Spells Hoodoos & Voodoos**

133'.4

For free catalog write:
Global Communications
P.O. Box 753
New Brunswick, NJ 08903

Free Subscription to Conspiracy Journal E-Mail Newsletter
www.conspiracyjournal.com

GYPSY WITCH PRESENTS: TROPICAL SPELLS HOODOOS & VOODOOS

Contents

The Hoodoo That You Do – By Dragonstar 5

Part One:
The Black Pullet, Or, The Hen With The Golden Eggs ……….. 8

Part Two:
What is Hoodoo? ……………………………………..... 68

Part Three:
Hoodoo Spells For Every Occasion ……………………….. 77

Part Four:
Conjure Powers with the Bible …………………………….. 86

Part Five:
Hoodoo with the Psalms ………………………………….. 107

Part Six:
How to Make a Mojo/Gris Gris Bag ……………………….. 127

Part Seven:
Hoodoo Rootworking …………………………………….. 138

GYPSY WITCH PRESENTS:
TROPICAL SPELLS HOODOOS & VOODOOS

GYPSY WITCH PRESENTS:
TROPICAL SPELLS HOODOOS & VOODOOS

That Hoodoo That You Do...
By Dragonstar

Ancient mysticism teaches that space-time and consciousness are polar aspects of each other. The entire field of space-time is like a reversed image of consciousness; matter is literally mind-stuff. This is the subject-object polarity. Just as on the objective side the universe is an unending process of space-time continuum, so also on the subjective side pure consciousness is an unceasing stream of self-transcendence.

Individual consciousness has a depth of extension equal to that of the universe itself. As incredible as this may seem, it is a very real metaphysical reality, the depth of space is a direct reflection of the depth of consciousness. The dimension of depth-consciousness is transcendental, and we do not see its magnitude of extension as such. It is like viewing a line end-on, appearing as a singularity in three-dimensional space, with the length of the line not perceived at all. Indeed, this dimension cannot be seen because it is what we see with, it is experienced as the force of consciousness, life itself.

The polarity of consciousness is the very same polarity that we experience as time, and space is its polar aspect projected outward. In other words: we do not live in time, but time lives within us; because time is the innermost rhythm of our conscious existence, which appears outside of ourselves as space. We could also say: Space is the possibility of movement, time the actuality or the realization of movement.

With this ancient understanding of space, time, and consciousness firmly in mind, we can look at the Big Bang in a different light. From a mystical perspective, the Big Bang of modern cosmology is a continuous process, an omnipresent condition which has always been the same no matter what we believed.

Western science, caught up in its purely objective view of existence, has imposed the concept of "universal time" on this timeless condition, projecting it into the past. Mankind has completely ignored the ancient message of non-dualistic mysticism resulting in our science of the universe being bogged down in the "strangeness" of relativity and quantum theory for most of this century.

We have certainly developed an extraordinary understanding of the physical universe, and this was no doubt the purpose of

GYPSY WITCH PRESENTS:
TROPICAL SPELLS HOODOOS & VOODOOS

modern science, but perhaps now is a good time to reintegrate the sacred science of the ancients. Best of all, a mystical understanding of modern cosmology sheds a good deal of light on the strange aspects of both modern physics and ancient mysticism.

Because of our direct connection with the universe and reality, our consciousness can subtly influence the day to day activities that normally seem beyond our control. For most of us our minds are wild and undisciplined. Our thoughts shoot from one subject to another with little or no conscious constraint. However, our thoughts are actually governing our reality and what will occur in our lives. Because most of our thoughts are chaotic and random, so too are our daily lives. We can be the masters of our destiny; it just takes a little will-power and self-discipline.

What these forms of magickal systems are trying to teach us is that everything in life is only as difficult as you think it is. As one grows in self-awareness, the realization slowly unfolds that one's own condition is brought about by oneself and one's own choices in life, whether they are gut reactive, knee-jerk choices or conscious choices. Whatever you were dealt with at birth, your choices throughout your life determine your outcome. The more complete the usage of both your mind and body, the more physically and mentally able you become, and the better you feel about yourself. Your words influence your thoughts. By thoughts we attune ourselves. The rule of the game is: **thoughts are reality**.

This is the great secret of the ancient Adepts. The hidden knowledge of hoodoo and rootwork reveals that consciousness is the ultimate energy in the universe. With this energy anything is possible. This is not as difficult as it appears; all we have to do is wake up.

The first part of this amazing book consists of the secret manuscript called *The Black Pullet*. This manuscript was fundamental in the development of what we know today as *Hoodoo*, or *Rootwork*. Other types of magickal systems, such as Pow-Wow and Folk-Magick were also greatly influenced by *The Black Pullet*.

The Black Pullet (La poule noire) is a grimoire that proposes to teach the "science of magical talismans and rings," including the art of necromancy and Kabbalah. It is believed to have been written in the 18th century by an anonymous French officer who served in Napoleon's army.

The text takes the form of a narrative centering on the French officer during the Egyptian expedition led by Napoleon (referred to here as the "genius") when his unit is suddenly attacked by Arab soldiers (Bedouins). The French officer manages

GYPSY WITCH PRESENTS:
TROPICAL SPELLS HOODOOS & VOODOOS

to escape the attack, but is the only survivor. An old Turkish man appears suddenly from the pyramids and takes the French officer into a secret apartment within one of the pyramids. He nurses him back to health whilst sharing with him the magical teachings from ancient manuscripts that escaped the "burning of Ptolemy's library."

The Black Pullet contains information regarding the creation of certain magical properties, such as talismanic rings, amulets and the Black Pullet itself. The book also teaches the reader how to master the extraordinary powers from these magical properties.

Perhaps the most interesting magical property claimed in the book is the power to produce the Black Pullet, otherwise known as the Hen that lays Golden Eggs. The grimoire claims that the person who understands and attains the power to instruct the Black Pullet will gain unlimited wealth. The notion of such a lucrative possession has been reflected throughout history in fables, fairy tales and folklore.

This text has often been associated to two other texts, known as the *Red Dragon* (or The Grand Grimoire) and the *Black Screech Owl*. The latter is also confusingly known as *The Black Pullet or Treasure of the Old Man of the Pyramids*, and is in fact an alternate printing of the original Black Pullet with only slight changes. All three grimoires claim to possess the science of ancient magic.

GYPSY WITCH PRESENTS: TROPICAL SPELLS HOODOOS & VOODOOS

PART ONE
The Black Pullet,
Or, The Hen with the Golden Eggs

Comprising the Science of Magical Talismans and Rings; the art of Necromancy and the Kabbalah, for conjuring the aerial and infernal spirits, sylphs, undines, and gnomes; for acquiring knowledge of the secret sciences; for discovering treasures, for the gaining of power to command all beings, and for unmasking all evil spells and sorceries.

From the teachings of Socrates, Pythagoras, Plato, Zoroaster, son of the great Aromasis, and other philosophers whose manuscripts escaped the burning of Ptolemy's library, and translated from the language of the Magi and of the Hieroglyphs, by the Doctors Mizzaboula-Jabamia, Danhuzerus, Nehmahmian, Judahim, Eliaeb, and translated into French by A.J.S .D.R.L.G.F. in Egypt.

GYPSY WITCH PRESENTS: TROPICAL SPELLS HOODOOS & VOODOOS

PREFACE

The work which we offer to the public must not be confused with a collection of reveries and errors to which their authors have tried to give credence by announcing supernatural feats; which the credulous and the ignorant seized with avidity. We only quote the most respectable authorities and most dignified in faith. The principles which we present are based on the doctrines of the ancients and modern, who full of respect for the Divinity, were always the friends of mankind, endeavored to recall them to virtue, by showing them vice in all its deformity.

We have drawn from the most pure sources, having only in view the love of truth and the desire to enlighten those who desire to discover the secrets of Nature and the marvels which they unfold to those who never separate the darkness which surrounds them. It is only given to those who are favored by The Great Being, to raise themselves above the terrestrial sphere, and to plan a bold flight in the etheric regions; it is for these privileged men that we write.

To us no importance is given to the splenetic Voices which are raised against us. The silence and the smile of disdain will be the only answer with which we shall oppose them, and we shall follow with firm Sustained steps the route which indicates to us the luminous stars which fill the heavens, which cover our heads, and which light these thousands of worlds, which bless every day with our Sovereign Master of the Universe, which He has created, also ourselves, and whose Will maintains this admirable order, which commands our admiration, our respect and our love.

GYPSY WITCH PRESENTS: TROPICAL SPELLS HOODOOS & VOODOOS

THE BLACK PULLET

Before beginning the subject, and to acquaint my readers of this profound Science, which until the present day has been the object of research of the most constant and profound meditations, I must unbosom myself how these marvelous secrets were communicated to me, and the manner in which the

Divine Providence allowed me to escape from the greatest dangers and, so to speak, conducted me by the Divine Hand, to prove that by Divine Will it is sufficient to raise unto Himself the last of Beings or to precipitate to naught those who are clothed with all power on Earth. We all therefore come from God, God is everything, and without God nothing can exist. Who more than I may penetrate the truth eternal and sacred.

I formed part of the expedition to Egypt, an officer in the army of the genius. I took part in the successes and reverses of this army, which victorious or obliged to cede to force from the eventualities and circumstances always covered itself with glory.

As there is no point in relating here any detail which deals with this memorable campaign, I will but relate one single feature, with which I was touched, and is necessary for the development which I must give to those whom I mentioned in my preface. I had been sent by the General, under whose orders I found myself, to draw up the plans of the Pyramids; he had given me an escort of some mounted light infantry horse.

I arrived with them at my destination without experiencing any accident, also without noticing anything that could conjecture the fate that awaited us. We had dismounted near the Pyramids, our horses had been tethered; sitting on the sands we appeased the hunger that tormented us. French gaiety seasoned the food which composed our frugal meal. It was on the point of ending, and I was occupied with my work when all of a sudden a horde of desert Arabs fell on us. We did not have the time to place ourselves in a position of defense. The blows of swords descended upon us, the bullets whistled, and I received several wounds.

My unhappy companions were lying on the ground dead or expiring. Our cruel enemies after having removed our weapons and clothes disappeared with our horses with the speed of lightning. I remained for some time in a state of prostration, facing the sun. At last recovering some of my strength, I raised myself with pain. I had two sword cuts on the head, and one on the left arm. I looked around me. I saw nothing but corpses, a burning sky and arid sand in an immense desert and a frightening solitude. With but the hope

GYPSY WITCH PRESENTS:
TROPICAL SPELLS HOODOOS & VOODOOS

of a certain and cruel death, I resigned myself to saying goodbye to my country to my parents and to my friends. Invoking heaven, I crawled to the Pyramid, and the blood which ran with abundance from my wounds reddened the sand which was soon to be my tomb.

Arriving at the foot of these worldly marvels I sat down and leaned against this enormous mass that had seen many centuries pass by and which would see many more pass. I thought that my existence which was soon to end had come to naught just as the day which was nearing its end, the sun being on the point of plunging into the ocean.

"Brilliant star, receive my goodbyes," I said with emotion. "My eyes will never see you again, your beneficent light will never shine on me again. Goodbye."

As I said this goodbye which I thought was eternal, the sun disappeared. The night came and covered the world with its dark curtain. I was absorbed with the most sad reflections when a light noise could be heard a few paces from me. A large slab of stone detached itself from the pyramid and fell on the sand; I turned to that side, and by the light of a small lantern that he carried in his hand, I perceived a venerable old man who came out of the pyramid. A white beard covered his chest, a turban covered his head, and the rest of his costume indicated that he was a Mohammedan. He cast his eyes around; then advancing a few steps he halted opposite the corpse of one of my unhappy companions of misfortune.

"Oh Heavens!" he cried in Turkish. "A man is wounded, a Frenchman is dead."

He lifted his eyes to the sky saying: "Oh Allah." He then discovered the others which he carefully examined to see if he could not find one who still breathed, and to assure himself, I saw him place his hand in the region of the heart. The old man recognized that they had all ceased to live. Uttering a painful groan, with tears furrowing down from his eyes, he retraced his steps to reenter the pyramid. I felt the desire to conserve my days. I had already made the sacrifice of my life; hope entered my heart. Summoning all my strength, I called to him; he heard me, and turning his lantern in my direction, he saw me. Advancing he gave me his hand, which I seized and pressed to my ups. He saw that I was wounded and that blood was flowing from the cuts on my head.

Placing his lantern on the ground, he removed his girdle and covered my brow. He then helped me to get up. I had lost a lot of

GYPSY WITCH PRESENTS: TROPICAL SPELLS HOODOOS & VOODOOS

blood and was suffering from extreme weakness—I hardly had the strength to support myself. Placing his lantern in my hand, and then taking me in his arms, he carried me near the opening in the pyramid from which he had come and placed me gently on the sand. Giving me an affectionate grip of the hand, he indicated that he was re-entering the pyramid and would return promptly.

I gave thanks to Heaven for the unexpected help that had been sent me. The old man reappeared carrying a flagon. He removed the cork and poured a few drops of the liqueur into a drinking vessel which he gave to me to drink. A delicious perfume diffused around me. Hardly had this Divine Liqueur penetrated my stomach than I felt regenerated, and I had enough strength to enter the pyramid with my benefactor and generous conductor.

We then stopped for a few moments. He replaced the stone that had fallen, which he adjusted with an iron bar, and we descended by an easy slope into the interior of the pyramid. After having walked for some time on the same path, which made several sinuous turns, we arrived at a door which he secretly opened and closed with care. Then having crossed an immense hall, we entered another place. A lamp hung from the ceiling; there was a table covered with books, several oriental divans or seats, and a bed on which to rest. The kind old man conducted me to a seat where he made me sit down. Placing his lantern on the table he opened a kind of cupboard from which he took several vases.

He approached me and invited me to remove my clothes with an attention and complaisance difficult to describe. Having examined my wounds he applied with solemn formality several balms which came from the vases of which I have previously spoken. Hardly had they been applied to my arms and head than the pains were soothed. He invited me to lie on his bed, and very soon a beneficial and soothing sleep weighed down my eyelids.

When I awoke, I looked around and saw sitting near me the good old man who did not wish to partake of rest while I was asleep as he feared that I might need help. I tendered him my most grateful thanks by the most expressive signs. In the same manner he signified to me that I must remain quiet. He gave me a new portion of the cordial which had already proved its happy effects. Afterwards he looked at me with extreme attention, and realizing that he had nothing to fear for my life, he affectionately patted my hand.

He then lay down on some cushions on the other side of the chamber where we were, and soon I heard him sleeping profoundly and peacefully.

GYPSY WITCH PRESENTS:
TROPICAL SPELLS HOODOOS & VOODOOS

"Oh benevolent one," I said to myself, "thou art virtue par excellance and a pure emanation of the Divinity; thou unitest and bringest men together and thou makest them forget the pains to which they are prey. Through thee they are returned to happiness, and too thou art this happiness, the object of all their wishes and all their desires."

My host made a movement and got up. He came to me and smiled at seeing me in a state of calm and tranquility which left him in no fear of my being. He gave me to understand that he was going to leave me so that he could go out of the pyramid and see what was happening outside. He brought to my side that which he thought would be necessary for my needs, and then he left me alone.

Until this moment I had not reflected at all on what had happened to me in this exigency. I found myself safe in this subterranean place, and I had no uneasiness relative to my host; however, this would have to come to an end by my departing after I had been cured and re-joining the Army.

I was occupied with these ideas when I saw the old man reenter. He gave me to understand that several Arab corps and Mamelouks were surveying the plain and that he had seen them without being noticed because his retreat was impenetrable to all eyes. He indicated that he had me in his care and regarded me as his son; therefore I could deliver myself to the greatest security.

I indicated to him my complete gratitude, and he appeared satisfied. As I appeared to be dissatisfied to be able to express myself only by signs, he brought me a book indicating that with its help we could soon communicate together without hesitation. The career which I had followed since my childhood had familiarized me with meditation, I loved the application of mind, and I was soon in the condition to listen to my generous old man. He also showed such compliance in the lessons which he gave me that even with less good will, one would have made progress. I remain silent on all that was relative to my new education.

My complete cure and convalescence took longer than I realized. My host went out from time to time to see what was taking place as he was in complete ignorance of earthly events.

In short, one day he was longer than usual, and on his return he informed me that the French Army had evacuated Egypt and that I could not hope to leave at this time without giving an account of the days that I had spent with him. I should stay with him which he would make me do by his kindness and love so that in my particular case of captivity my fate would not be as cruel as I

GYPSY WITCH PRESENTS:
TROPICAL SPELLS HOODOOS & VOODOOS

might think because he would teach me things which would astonish me and I should desire nothing in the way of good fortune.

I had begun to understand the Turkish language. He told me to get up. I obeyed him. He took me by the hand and conducted me to the end of the chamber. He opened a door opposite the one by which one entered, and taking a lamp from the table we entered a vault where there were disposed in regular lines several coffers which he opened. They were full of gold and gems of every kind.

"You see my son that with this one never fears poverty. Everything is yours; I am reaching the end of my career, and I shall be happy to leave them in your possession. These treasures are not the fruit of avarice and a sordid interest. I own them by the knowledge of Occult Sciences with which I am familiar and the boon which has been granted to me by The Great Being to penetrate the secrets of Nature. I can still command the Powers that populate the Earth and Space and are not visible to ordinary men.

"I like you, my dear son. I recognize in you the candor, sincerity, love of truth, and aptitude for these sciences, and most of all I wish you to know that they have cost me more than eighty years of research, meditation, and experience.

"The science of the Magicians, the language of the hieroglyphics, has been lost by the downfall of man. Only I am the guardian. I will impart these precious confidences to you, and we will read together these characters traced on the pyramids which have been the despair of scholars and before which they have paled for many centuries."

The prophetic manner in which he spoke impressed me and I showed a very lively desire to understand that with which he wished to acquaint me. I told him this in the Turkish language which I was beginning to understand and to talk in a manner so that I could be understood.

"Your wishes shall be fulfilled," answered my adopted father.

Then lifting one hand to the arch of heaven, he spoke in a solemn tone: *"Love, my son, love the very good and the very grand God of the philosophers, and never become proud if he brings you in contact with the children of wisdom for you to associate in their company and to make you a participant in the wonders of his power."*

After having finished this invocation of sorts, he then said while looking at me: "Such are the principles which you must fathom. Try and make yourself worthy to receive the light. The hour

GYPSY WITCH PRESENTS:
TROPICAL SPELLS HOODOOS & VOODOOS

of your regeneration has come. You will become like a new individual.

"Pray fervidly to Him who alone has the power to create new hearts, to give you that which will make you capable of great things that I have to teach you, and to inspire me to withhold from you none of the mysteries of Nature. Pray. Hope. I eulogize the eternal wisdom which has been placed in my soul and wish to disclose to you its ineffable truths. And you will be lucky, my son, if nature has placed in your soul the resolution that these high mysteries will demand of you. You will learn to command all Nature.

"God alone will be your master, and the enlightened Will alone be your equal. The supreme intelligences will glory in obeying your desires. The Demons will not dare to be found where you are. Your voice will make them tremble in the pits of the abyss, and all the invisibles who inhabit the four elements will esteem themselves happy to administer to your pleasures. I adore you oh Great God for having enthroned man with so much glory, and having established him as sovereign monarch of all the works made by your hands. Do you feel, my son, do you feel this heroic ambition which is the sure stamp of the children of wisdom? Do you dare to desire to serve only the one God and to dominate over all that is not God? Have you understood what it is to prove to be a man and to be unwilling to be a slave since you are born to be a Sovereign? And if you have these noble thoughts, as the signs which I have found on your physiognomy do not permit me to doubt, have you considered maturely whether you have the courage and the strength to renounce all the things which could possibly be an obstacle to attaining the greatness for which you have been born?"

At this point he stopped and regarded me fixedly as if waiting for an answer, or as if he were searching to read my heart.

I asked him, "What is that which I have to renounce?"

"All that is evil in order to occupy yourself only with that which is good. The proneness with which nearly all of us are born to vice rather than to virtue. Those passions which render us slaves to our senses which prevent us from applying ourselves to study, tasting its sweetness, and gathering its fruits. You see, my dear son, that the sacrifice which I demand of you is not painful and is not above your powers; on the contrary, it will make you approach perfection as near as it is possible for man to attain. Do you accept that which I propose?"

"Oh my Father," I answered, "nothing conforms more to my

GYPSY WITCH PRESENTS:
TROPICAL SPELLS HOODOOS & VOODOOS

desires that that one should choose propriety and virtue."

"It suffices," answered the old man. "Before unfolding to you completely the doctrine which will initiate you into the mysteries, which are most profound and the most sacred, you must understand that the elements are inhabited by very perfect creatures. The immense space between Heaven and Earth has inhabitants far more noble than the birds and the gnats. The vast seas have many other hosts than the whales and dolphin. It is the same in the depths of the earth which contains other things than water and minerals, and the element of fire, more noble than the other three, has not been created to abide there useless and empty. The air is full of an unnumbered multitude of beings with human form—a little proud in appearance but in effect docile and great lovers of the sciences; subtle but obliging to the great Mages and enemies of the foolish and the ignorant: these are the sylphs. The seas and rivers are the habitat of the Ondines, the Earth is full practically to the center of Gnomes, guardians of the treasures and the precious stones. These are the ingenious friends of man and easy to command. They supply to the children of the Magicians all moneys of which they have need and only ask payment for their services in the glory of being commanded.

"As for the Salamanders, the inhabitants of the fire regions, they serve the philosophers, but they do not seek the attention of their company.

"I could also talk about the familiar spirits: Socrates, as well as Pythagoras and a few other wise men, had his. I have one also; he is near me when I have need of him. This will no doubt seem strange to you, but even if your eyes do not convince you of the truth, you will be able to believe it if you have any confidence in Socrates, Plato, Pythagoras, Zoroaster, Proclus, Porphyry, Iamblichus, Ptolemy, Trismegistus and other wise men to whose enlightenment one must add those who give us the natural knowledge.

"It remains for me to speak to you of the Talismans, those magic circles, which will give you the power to command all the elements, to avoid all the dangers, all the snares of your enemies, and to assure you the success of all your enterprises and the fulfillment of your wishes."

He arose, opened a chest which was at the foot of his bed, and took out a cedarwood box covered in gold veneer and enriched with diamonds of an extraordinary brilliance. The lock on which were engraved hieroglyphic characters was also of gold. He opened this casket, and I saw a large quantity of talismans and rings which were enriched with diamonds and engraved with

GYPSY WITCH PRESENTS:
TROPICAL SPELLS HOODOOS & VOODOOS

magical and cabalistic symbols. It was impossible to look at them without being dazzled.

"You see, my son, each one has its virtue, its peculiar virtue, but to make use of it you must understand the language of the Magicians in order to pronounce the mysterious words engraved thereon. I will teach them to you before working with you on the great performance with the spirits and the animals who are submissive to my authority and who obey me blindly.

"You will see when you have been initiated into all these mysteries of how many errors the majority of those who pretend to be servile to nature have been guilty. They love the truth and believe they have discovered it by means of abstract ideas and lose their way in the faith of a reason of which they do not know the limits.

"The vulgar or common people do not see over the world in which they live other than an arch of glittering light during the day and a scattering of stars during the night. These are the limited ones of the universe. Certain of the philosophers have seen more and have increased (their knowledge) up to nearly the present time to the point of affrighting our imagination. Further, what prodigious work is offered at one stroke to the human spirit! Employ eternity even to survey it; take the wings of dawn, fly to the planet Saturn in the skies which extend over this planet. You will find without ceasing new spheres, new orbs, and worlds accumulating one above another. You will find infinity in matter, in space, in movement, in the number of nuances and shades which adorn them. As our souls expand with our ideas and assimilate in a certain manner the objects which they penetrate, how much then must a man become elated at having penetrated the inconceivable profundities? I am an upstart thanks to wisdom, and you will reach this point too."

He arose and took up several manuscripts which were on the table.

"These precious books, my dear son, will acquaint you with things unknown to the rest of humanity and which will seem never to have existed. These books escaped the fire of the library of Ptolemy. They have received some damage, as you see; in effect, several pages have been blackened by the fire.

"Ah well! It is by the knowledge which I have been able to draw from these works that I have the authority to command all the beings who inhabit the aerial and terrestrial regions, known and unknown to man.

"Oh my son! Prostrate yourself before the Divinity, deplore in His presence the errors of the human spirit, and promise Him to be

GYPSY WITCH PRESENTS:
TROPICAL SPELLS HOODOOS & VOODOOS

as virtuous as it is possible for a man to be. Guard against studying moral philosophy in the ignorant writings of the multitudes, in the schemes produced by the heat of the imagination, by the restlessness of the spirit, or by the desire for celebrity which torments their authors. Seek guidance in those works where, having no other interest than truth or other aim than public usefulness, they render to morals and to virtue the homage which they have deserved in all times and from all peoples."

I listened to this good old man with an admiration mixed with respect; he had stopped speaking and I thought I heard him still. A sweet majesty reigned in all his features, and the persuasion seemed to pour from his lips like a limpid stream running down a slope to fertilize the prairies. He noticed my admiration which was akin to ecstasy.

"My dear son," he said, "I pardon your astonishment. You have until now lived in the society of men who are corrupt, who have learnt to doubt everything and to forget the respect which one owes to Him who has brought forth all from nothing. Wisdom for them a meaningless difficulty, but as you learn it, it will become for you a practical virtue. You will look on it as something very simple, as natural to you as the air you breathe and as necessary to you for your existence. Your wounds are healing. Tomorrow I will commence your education in wisdom, and I will give you the first lesson. I am now going to my aviary to feed my prisoners."

"What!" I said to him. "Your prisoners! With your philosophy and the love of humanity which characterizes you, do you deprive living creatures of their liberty?"

He smiled at my observation.

"My dear son, that which I do is necessary to facilitate my mysterious operations, but the destiny of those submissive to my laws is perhaps sweeter than if they enjoyed complete liberty. Besides, they have never known the prize and so cannot desire it. Tomorrow you will have the answer to all these enigmas.

He then left me to enter the cave where he had led me when he showed me the chests filled with gold and precious stones. Soon he came back. I got up. He told me to approach the awning so that we could eat something before going to sleep. He picked up the papers that were on the table. He took a seat and told me to sit by his side. I obeyed, but as I did not see any food, he laughingly added that this food was not very substantial but that in a moment I would see that he had cooks and slaves equally clever and intelligent. He immediately pronounced these words: *Ag, Gemenos, Tur, Nicophanta,* and blew three times on a ring which he had on his finger. Immediately the place was lit up by seven chandeliers of rock crystal which appeared from the void.

Nine slaves entered bringing various viands on golden plates and wine in vessels of the greatest richness. Incense burned in tripods, and celestial music could be heard. Everything was placed on the table in the most beautiful order, and the slaves stood to attention around us to serve.

"You see, my son," the good old man repeated to me, "I have but to command to be obeyed. Eat, serve yourself, and choose what will gratify you."

Everything which I tasted was delicious. Then I took my goblet, and the wine, like nectar, which had been poured into it, its bouquet forerunner to its delicate taste, appealed agreeably to my sense of smell.

When it had astonished my pallet and I had relished it, it seemed as though a divine fire flowed through my veins and as if I had acquired a new existence. I looked at the slaves who served us; they were all in the flower of their youth, of the greatest beauty, and dressed in rose silk tunics with white belts. They had flowing golden curls waving on their shoulders. With lowered eyes of respect, they attended to the orders of their master.

The old man allowed me to finish my survey, and he then followed up with: "My son you have appeased your hunger?" "Yes, my Father." He raised his hand and said: *Osuam, Bedac, Acgos,* and the slaves hurried to remove all that was on the table. They went out, the chandeliers disappeared, and two beds arranged themselves on each side of the apartment which was no longer lit except for the lamp that cast a soft light not unlike twilight.

"There, my dear son, is the manner in which you will be served every day. Your occupations will vary innumerably and thus will preserve you from tediousness. Deliver yourself to sleep, I will do the same, and tomorrow when day appears, I will keep my word which I have given to you."

"But my Father, the daylight will never penetrate into your abode; how can you know when break of day will appear?"

"That depends on my will, my son; it is another surprise that I will arrange for you. Until tomorrow, sleep in peace."

He extended his hand to me, and I pressed it to my heart. He approached his bed, lay down and soon sleep weighed down his eyes. I imitated him for a little while after which I fell asleep.

Then I opened my eyes the lamp had vanished, daylight lit the chamber, and the rays of sun penetrated there. The old man was walking with a book in his hand. The movement that I made

GYPSY WITCH PRESENTS:
TROPICAL SPELLS HOODOOS & VOODOOS

interrupted his perusal. He looked at me smilingly. I got up hurriedly and flew into the arms he opened to me.

"My father, I salute you."

"You have rested well, my dear son," he said, as I judge by the calm which reigns on your countenance. Render homage to God who has permitted you to enjoy again this beautiful day, which lights you, and ere I initiate you into the mysteries of wisdom, I will have a conversation with you on a point of my doctrine which is necessary for developments."

He gave me a book and opening it said: "Here is the first page and the prayer which you must address to the Great Being."

And I read that which follows:

ORATION OF THE SAGES

Immortal, Eternal, Ineffable, and Sacred Father of all things, who is carried on the chariot rolling without cease, of the worlds which rotate always. Ruler of the Etheric Plain where Your throne of power is exalted and from whose heights Thy formidable eyes discover everything and Your beautiful and saintly ears hear everything. Harken to Your children whom You have loved from their birth through all time.

Since Your lasting, great, and eternal majesty shines brightly over the world and the starry heavens, Thou art raised above them. Oh, sparkling fire! There You light and maintain Yourself in the appropriate splendour. There comes forth from Your being never-failing streams of light which nourish Your infinite spirit. This infinite spirit generates all things and makes this inexhaustible treasure of matter which cannot fail to procreate that which always surrounds it because of the forms without number with which it is filled and with which You have filled it since the beginning of time. From this spirit the very saintly kings who are standing around Your throne and who compose Your court also draw their origin.

Oh, Universal Father! Oh, Unique One! Oh, Father of blissful mortals and immortals! You have particularly created the powers which are marvelously like Your eternal thought and Your adorable essence. You have established them superior to the angels who announce Your wishes to the world. Finally, You have created us sovereigns over the elements. Our continued exertion is to praise You and to adore Your desires. We burn with the desire to be possessed of You. Oh, Father! Oh, Mother, the most tender of Mothers! Oh, admirable example of tender sentiments of Mothers!

GYPSY WITCH PRESENTS:
TROPICAL SPELLS HOODOOS & VOODOOS

Oh, Son, the flower of all Sons! Oh, mold of all our shapes! Well beloved spirit, soul, harmony, and number of all things, we adore You.

When I had finished, he said to me: "My dear son, I have spoken to you of the spirits that populate the firmament, the sea, the Earth, and fire, that is to say the elements. I have spoken to you of the spirits and am going to go into greater detail to extend the limits of your intelligence and to give you the means of penetrating into and understanding the sacred mysteries which will be divulged to you.

"When the universe was full of life, this unique son, this God-engendered, had received a spherical body, the most perfect of all; he was subject to circular movement, the simplest of all, the most suitable to his shape. The Supreme Being surveyed his work with complaisance, and having compared it with the model which He followed in his operations, He recognized with pleasure that the principal traits of the original repeated themselves in the copy. He did not grant him eternity for these two worlds could not have the same perfections. He made time, the mobile image of immobile eternity, which measures the duration of the sensible world as eternity measures that of the intellectual world, and for that He left traces of his presence and his movements. The Supreme Being kindled the sun and cast him with the other planets into the vast solitude of the airs. It is from there that this heavenly body floods the sky with its light. The contriver of all things then addressed His commandment to the spirits to whom he had entrusted the administration of the heavenly bodies.

"Gods, who owe your birth to Me, listen to My sovereign commands. You do not have the right to immortality; but you participate in it by the power of My will, more powerful than the bonds which unite the parts of which you are composed. It remains for the perfection of all this to fill with inhabitants the seas, the Earth, and the airs. If they should owe the day to me immediately, escape the empire of death, they would become equal to the gods themselves. I thus lay on you the care of producing them. Agents of My power, unite to these perishable bodies the favor of immortality which you have received from my hand. Mold in particular those beings who command other animals and who are submissive to you; who are born by your orders; who increase by your good deeds, and who after their death are reunited with you and participate in your happiness.

"He spoke, and suddenly, pouring into the basin where he

GYPSY WITCH PRESENTS:
TROPICAL SPELLS HOODOOS & VOODOOS

had kneaded the Soul of the World the remainder of this Soul held in reserve, he then fashioned the individual Souls, and joining to those of men a small portion of the Divine Essence, he attached to them irrevocable destinies. Finally, having appointed to the inferior gods the successive reclothement of mortal bodies to provide for and control their needs, the Supreme Being reentered into eternal rest. The inferior gods were obliged to employ the same means in developing us and thus the maladies of the body and the even more dangerous ones of the soul. All that is good in the universe in general and in man in particular derives from the Supreme God; all that is defective comes from the vices inherent in matter.

"The Earth and the heavens are populated, my dear son, with Spirits to whom the Supreme Being has confided the administration of the Universe; He has distributed them everywhere nature appears to be animated but principally in those regions which stretch around and above us from the earth up to the sphere of the Moon. It is there where an immense authority is exercised, they dispensing life and death, the good and the bad, light and darkness.

"Each nation, each individual finds in these invisible representatives an ardent friend to protect him, an enemy no less ardent to pursue him. They are clothed in an aerial body; their essence holds the middle between Divine Nature and nature; they surpass us in intelligence; some of them are subject to our passions, mostly in the changes which pass them on to a superior rank. Because of their innumerable multitude, spirits are divided into four classes: the first of perfect beings whom the common herd adore and who reside in the stars; the second, those of the spirits properly called and of whom I conversed with you; the third, those beings less perfect who however, render great service to humanity; the fourth, those of our souls, after they have been separated from the bodies which they inhabited. We may discern from the first three the honors which will one day become part of our nature if we cultivate exclusively wisdom and virtue.

"To render you more sensible of that which I have put forward to you relative to the spirits, I will give you an account of what befell me with those who are submissive to me. Know also that they only communicate to souls after a long time of preparation in meditation and prayer. The dominion which I have obtained over my spirit is the result of my constancy in the practice of the virtues. In the beginning I saw him only rarely; one day yielding to my repeated entreaties he transported me to the realm of the spirits. Listen, my son, to the story of my voyage.

GYPSY WITCH PRESENTS:
TROPICAL SPELLS HOODOOS & VOODOOS

"The moment of departure having arrived, I felt my soul detach itself from the bonds which attached it to the body, and I found myself in the middle of a new world of animated substances, good or malignant, blithe or sad, prudent or careless. We followed them for some time, and I thought I recognized some who were directing the interests of nations and those of individuals, the researches of sages and the opinions of the multitude.

"Soon a woman of gigantic stature extended her black veils over the vault of the skies; and having descended slowly to Earth, she gave her orders to the cortege which had accompanied her. We glided into several houses. Sleep and its ministers scattered poppies with full hands; and while silence and peace spread gently around virtuous men, remorse's and frightful specters shook the beds of the wicked with violence.

"'Dawn and the hours open the barriers of the day,' my guide said to me. 'It is time to rise into the air. See the tutelary spirits of Egypt soaring over the different towns and regions which the Nile irrigates. They dispel as much as possible the evils with which they are menaced; nevertheless, their countryside will be devastated because the spirits enveloped in dark clouds are advancing and thundering against us; he then announced to me the arrival of the army of which you formed a part because he had knowledge of its coming.

"'Observe now these assiduous agents, who, with a flight as rapid and as restless as the swallow, skim over the earth and cast piercing looks on all sides for greed and avidity; these are the inspectors of human affairs. Some spread their sweet influence over the mortals whom they protect; others launch the relentless Nemesis against grave transgressions. See these mediators, these expounders who rise and descend without cease; they carry your prayers and your offerings to the gods; they bring back to us happy or distressing dreams and the secrets of the future which are then revealed to you by the mouth of the oracles.'"

"Oh my protector!" I cried suddenly, "here are beings which in their stature and sinister appearance inspire terror; they come to us.

"'Flee,' he said to me, 'they are unhappy, the good fortune of others irritates them, and they spare only those who pass their life in sufferings and in tears.'

"Escaping from their fury, we found objects no less afflicting. Discord, the detestable and eternal source of dissentions which torment men, marched proudly above their heads and whispered outrage and vengeance into their hearts. With timid steps and

GYPSY WITCH PRESENTS:
TROPICAL SPELLS HOODOOS & VOODOOS

lowered eyes, the prayers trailed on their steps and endeavored to recall everywhere the calm they had showed themselves. Glory was pursued by envy who tore her own sides; truth by imposters who changed its face from moment to moment; each virtue by several vices which carried snares or knives.

"Fortune appeared suddenly. My guide said to me, 'You can speak with her.' I felicitated her on the gifts which she distributed to mortals. She told me in a serious tone that she did not give but took a great interest. While uttering these words, she soaked the flowers and fruits which she held in one hand in a poisoned cup which she held in the other.

"Then passed near us two powerful spirits who left long trails of light after them. The one was war and the other wisdom.

"My guide told me two armies were approaching each other and were on the point of coming to blows. Wisdom would place herself near the general whose cause was just and he would be the victor because worth must triumph.

"'Let us leave these unhappy spheres,' said my spirit. We leapt the limits of the sphere of darkness and death with the speed of lightning and of thought. We then shot above the sphere of the Moon, and we reached the regions lit by eternal day.

'Let us stop for an instant,' said my guide. 'Cast your eyes over the magnificent spectacle which surrounds you; listen to the divine harmony which is produced by the regular movement of the celestial bodies; look how to each planet, each star, is attached a spirit which directs its course. These heavenly bodies are populated by sublime intelligences of a nature superior to ours.'

"With my eyes fixed on the sun, I contemplated with ravishment the spirit who with a vigorous arm pushes this scintillating globe on the course which he has decreed. I watched him cast aside with fury the souls who endeavored to plunge into the boiling surges of this sphere to purify themselves although they were not worthy of this blessing. Touched by their misfortune, I begged my conductor to take me away from this sight and to lead me into the distance towards an enclosure where one could escape the rays of light which were too brilliant. I hoped to catch a glimpse of the Sovereign of the Universe surrounded by the assistants of His throne and of those pure beings who our philosophers call numbers, eternal ideas or spirits of the mortals. My spirit told me that the Sovereign inhabits regions inaccessible to humans, that we should offer him our homage and descend to Earth."

Hardly had he spoken when we found ourselves in the same

GYPSY WITCH PRESENTS:
TROPICAL SPELLS HOODOOS & VOODOOS

place from whence we had made our departure.

He said to me, "I have let you become acquainted with that which no mortal has ever been permitted to glimpse. From this moment it is no longer forbidden to me to hide anything from you.' And he unveiled to me all the mysteries in which I will let you participate. To convince you of the truth of all that I have given out to you, you will see my spirit, who will become yours since I have adopted you as my son. He will see in you another me."

He pronounced these two words: *Koux, Ompax*. In that instant I saw appear a young man of the most beautiful stature; the remainder of his person shone with all the charms, and on the summit of his head shone a flame of which my eyes could not sustain the brilliance. He said smiling at the old man: *Oles, Nothos, Perius*. The old man took his hand and answered: *Solathas, Zanteur, Dinanteur*. The spirit then stood by his side.

The old man noticed that the spirit's light dazzled my eyes. "When you have been initiated into the mysteries of wisdom, you will be able to contemplate this fire without danger and even to stand the rays of the sun. Let us begin the initiation, let us stand."

I executed this order which he had given as did the spirit. He placed his hand on my head and said: "*Sina, Misas, Tanaim, Orsel, Misanthos.*" A voice which came from the cavern wherein were the coffers containing all the precious stones gave this answer: "*Torzas, Elicanthus, Orbitau.*"

Hardly had the last word been pronounced than we found ourselves in the most profound darkness. The fire which shone on the head of the spirit had also disappeared.

"Be without dread or fear," the old man said.

"My father, am I not with you?"

"Your answer pleases me, it proclaims confidence. You will now test the effects of it."

He then said: "*Thomatos, Benasser, Elianter.*"

Everything was then lit up but by a seemingly dark light, and I saw enter several individuals who took up positions around the room.

"Here are all the spirits who will be subservient to you; I will proclaim them to you."

He took me by the hand and conducted me around the room. He stopped in front of every spirit and said to me: "Repeat with me: *Litau, Izer, Osnas.*"

I obeyed and each spirit bowed saying, "*Nanther.*"

There were thirty-three. When we had reached the last one, he told me to return to the place which I had occupied. Then he

GYPSY WITCH PRESENTS:
TROPICAL SPELLS HOODOOS & VOODOOS

took a wand six feet in length having at one end the head of a serpent and at the other the tail. On the wand were plates of gold the same as the head and tail on which were engraved the characters as illustrated in Figure 1. He formed a circle by uniting each end by a golden chain which he passed through two links; he put it on the ground and placed himself in the center.

No. 1
Figure of the Wand stained with blood of the lamb.

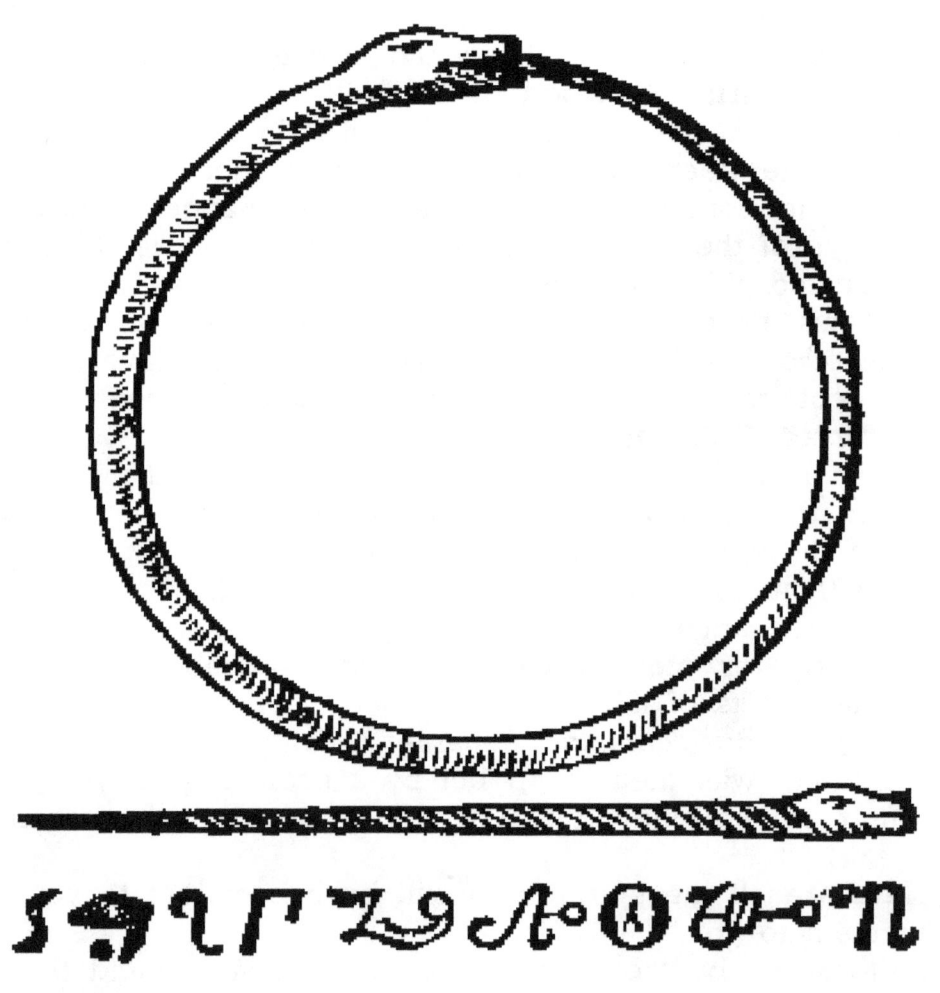

These characters should be written on the wand with India ink.

GYPSY WITCH PRESENTS:
TROPICAL SPELLS HOODOOS & VOODOOS

"What do you wish to see at this moment, my son?" he asked me.

"The plain on which you found me at the point of death from pain and want," I answered.

He raised his hands toward heaven and said, "*Soutram, Ubarsinens.*"

Immediately the spirits approached me and taking me in their arms, they lifted me, and I found myself transported to the foot of the Pyramid. I saw a multitude of Arabs on horseback who were surveying it. Although I had not noticed him, the old man was near me enjoying my astonishment.

"You see, my son, how all the spirits are submissive to you, how they will obey you and await your orders. Do you wish to return to the place which you left or to soar for some time in the middle of the aerial parts? Do you know that you can see all that is happening around you and that you are visible only to the Great Being who wishes to accord you wisdom and to those who accompany you?"

I testified to the desire to survey the immensity.

"Pronounce Saram while extending your arms towards the east, and you will be satisfied."

I uttered this word and made the indicated sign. The spirits lifted me up as well as the old man. We approached the clouds, and the vast horizon opened to my enchanted eyes. The old man once again said to me: "You see I have not made vain promises, you will have the same success in all your undertakings, but let us return to the Pyramid. The spirits await us, and we will continue our workings."

He said "*Rabiam*," and very soon we reentered the abode of the old man.

When we were seated, the spirits disappeared, only the first one remaining with us. All the insignia were changed, and a very intense light illuminated the vault. He then formed the second Magic Circle.

Placing himself therein, the old man said to me: "Go near your spirit. I give you permission for I know that you have a pure heart that you have never been guilty of any action which would make you blush. If that were not the case, you would be struck down dead on entering this circle. Go, my son."

I followed his instructions. He opened the casket where all the rings were to be found, and drew out that one shown in figure 3 as well as the talisman which he placed in my hands.

GYPSY WITCH PRESENTS:
TROPICAL SPELLS HOODOOS & VOODOOS

No. 2

No. 3

GYPSY WITCH PRESENTS: TROPICAL SPELLS HOODOOS & VOODOOS

"This one will serve to conjure the celestial and infernal powers. Put the ring on your finger and the talisman over your heart, then pronounce the following words: *Siras, Etar, Besanar*, and you will perceive the effects."

Hardly had these words come from my mouth than I saw a multitude of spirits and figures of different shapes. The spirit who was at my side said to me: "Command and order and your desires will be satisfied."

The old man added, "My son, the sky and the hells are at your orders. I think that at this moment you are not in want of anything; therefore, if you believe me, put off until later proving the Intelligence and activity of these spirits. To make them disappear, remove the ring from your finger and the talisman from the place which it occupies, and they will return to their sphere."

I did that which he ordered me to do, and they all went like a dream.

"There remain many things for me to teach you to make you at ease with these rings and talismans. This instruction will be the object of very important work which we shall do together with the help of our spirit.

"Let us follow the course of our experiences. Stay where you are."

He gave me another ring and talisman (Figure No. 4).

"These two precious objects, my son, are destined to make you loved by the most beautiful portion of the human race. There is not a woman who would not be happy to please you and who would not employ all possible means to be successful at it. Do you wish the most beautiful odalisque of the Grand Caliph should be brought before you in an instant? Put the ring on the second finger of your left hand, press the talisman against your lips, and say tenderly in a whisper: "*Nades, Suradis, Manier.*" Suddenly a spirit with rose-colored wings appeared; he placed himself on his knees before me.

"He awaits your orders," the old man said.

"Say to him: *Sader, Prostas, Solaster.*" I repeated these words, and the spirit vanished.

"He is now going to traverse an immense space with the rapidity of thought, and the most beautiful forms will appear right before your eyes that will serve as a model to paint those hour in which our Divine Prophet promises to his faithful servants. O my son, how blessed you are; not every mortal obtains from the Great Spirit such favors as I can see by the speed with which your wishes are executed."

GYPSY WITCH PRESENTS:
TROPICAL SPELLS HOODOOS & VOODOOS

No. 4

These characters should be engraved on the inside of the ring.

GYPSY WITCH PRESENTS:
TROPICAL SPELLS HOODOOS & VOODOOS

He had finished speaking when the spirit with the rose-colored wings arrived carrying in his arms a woman enveloped in a large white veil. She seemed to be asleep, and he placed her gently on a couch which appeared near me. He raised the veil which hid her. Never had anything so beautiful been offered to my eyes; she was Venus with all the charms of innocence. She sighed and opened the most beautiful eyes in the world which came to rest on me.

In a most harmonious voice she uttered a cry of surprise saying, "It is he."

The old man told me to approach the beauty, place a knee on the ground, for it is thus that one should speak to her, and to take her hand. I obeyed, and the divinity to whom I addressed my homage said to me: "I have seen thee in a dream, and the reality thereof makes thee more dear to my heart. I prefer you to the Sultan who for a long time has fatigued me with his homage."

"That is enough," said the old man, and he said forcefully, "Mammes Laher."

Four slaves appeared to remove the couch and she who had made such a vivid impression on my heart. The old man noticed my emotion and the pain which resulted from her departure.

He said to me, "You will see her again. Understand that in order to possess wisdom, it is necessary to know how to resist the allurements of voluptuousness."

His words made me come to myself, and I said to him, "Pardon, my father, but you have seen her, that is my excuse."

I replaced the ring and the talisman in the casket, and he gave me that which is illustrated in Figure No. 5.

"This talisman and this ring are not less valuable. They will enable you to discover all the treasures which exist and to ensure you the possession of them. Place the ring on the second finger of your right hand, enclose the talisman with the thumb and little finger of your left hand, and say, *Onaim, Perantes, Rasonastos*."

I repeated these three words, and seven spirits of a bronze color appeared, each carrying a large hide bag which they emptied at my feet. They contained gold coins which rolled in the middle of the hail where we were. I had not noticed that one of the spirits had on his shoulder a black bird, its head covered with a kind of hood.

GYPSY WITCH PRESENTS: TROPICAL SPELLS HOODOOS & VOODOOS

No. 5

These characters should be engraved on the inside of the ring.

GYPSY WITCH PRESENTS: TROPICAL SPELLS HOODOOS & VOODOOS

"It is this bird," the old man said to me, "who has made them find all this treasure. Do not think that these are some of what you have seen here. You can assure yourself of this."

I replied, "You are for me the truth itself. My father! Do you believe that I would insult you by doubting?"

He made a sign, and the spirits replaced the gold in the bags and disappeared.

"You see, my son, what the virtues of these talismans and rings are. When you know them all, you will be able, without my aid, to perform such miracles as you judge proper. Replace in the casket those of which you have made proof, and take this one (Figure No. 6).

"They will enable you to discover the most hidden secrets; you will be able to penetrate everywhere without being seen, and not a single word in the universe can be uttered without it coming to your ears, whether you wish to listen to it yourself or to have it brought back to us by your agents when you order them to do so. To prove it to you, repeat these words and place the talisman near your ear while you hold the ring tightly in your left hand: *Nitrae, Radou, Sunandam.*"

I distinctly heard a voice which said to me: "The Grand Mogul has decided in his private council that he must declare war on the Emperor of China."

Another voice said to me: "All is rumor in Constantinople. Last night the Sultana was carried off, and the Grand Sultan is in despair. He has had all the eunuchs thrown into the sea after having had them beheaded."

"Oh Heavens! What mischief I have done without wishing it," I cried in pain.

"Well, my son," the old man said, "It is a lesson for you to learn—not to be enslaved by your passions and to know how to curb them. This is enough for today, tomorrow we will continue."

The next day we followed the course of our mysterious operations. The spirit had not left us.

"You see, my son," said the old man, "that everything becomes easy with confidence and a pure soul without stain."

GYPSY WITCH PRESENTS: TROPICAL SPELLS HOODOOS & VOODOOS

No. 6

These characters should be engraved on the inside of the ring.

GYPSY WITCH PRESENTS:
TROPICAL SPELLS HOODOOS & VOODOOS

He opened the casket and took from it the talisman and ring (Figure No. 7).

When he had placed them in my hands, he pronounced two words, which I will teach you.

"Place this ring on the little finger of your left hand and the talisman to your right ear, and the most discreet man will divulge to you his most hidden thoughts. Here are the two words: *Noctar, Raiban*, and if you add a third word, which is *Biranther*, your greatest enemies will not be able to prevent themselves from loudly publishing their projects against you. In order to convince you, I am going to have appear before you one of the Beys of Cairo, and he will impart to you all of his schemes against the French."

He then said "*Nocdar*," to the spirit who then vanished like lightening. A quarter of an hour after he returned with the Bey who said: "We have made a treaty of alliance with the English, and the armistice concluded with the French will be broken without warning."

He disappeared with the spirit after the old man had said: "Zelander. The Mufti of the Grand Mosque will appear before your eyes and show you a manuscript of a work which he has composed and which he has refused to show to his best friends, even the Grand Visir."

I did that which has previously been indicated, and very soon the Mufti appeared and placing his manuscript on the table, he said to me: "*Tonas, Zugar*," which means in the language of the magi: <u>Read and Believe</u>.

The old man looked at him affectionately; he gave him his hand pronounced with sweetness and expression, *o Solem*. The Mufti, after bowing, disappeared.

"Return the talisman and the ring to me," the old man said, and take this." (Figure No. 8)

"It will serve to activate as many spirits as you wish to undertake or to stop operations which would be contrary to you. The magic words are: *Zorami, Zaitux, Elastot*. We will not at this moment make any experiments; tomorrow we will go to the shores of the Nile and we will have constructed a bridge of a single arch on which we shall pass to the other side of the river.

GYPSY WITCH PRESENTS:
TROPICAL SPELLS HOODOOS & VOODOOS

No. 7

These characters should be engraved on the inside of the ring.

GYPSY WITCH PRESENTS:
TROPICAL SPELLS HOODOOS & VOODOOS

No. 8

Characters to be engraved on the inside of the ring.

GYPSY WITCH PRESENTS:
TROPICAL SPELLS HOODOOS & VOODOOS

"Here is the next talisman and its ring (Figure No. 9). They have the property of destroying everything, of commanding the elements, of calling down the thunder, hail, the stars, earthquakes, hurricanes, water spouts on land and sea, and of preserving our friends from all accidents. Here are the words which one must pronounce (the numbers indicate each thing that you wish to operate): first, you pronounce: *Ditau, Hurandos*; second, *Ridas, Talimol*; third, *Atrosis, Narpida*; fourth, *Uusur, Itar*; fifth, *Hispen, Tromador*; sixth, *Paranthes, Histanos*."

No. 9

These characters should be engraved on the inside of the ring.

GYPSY WITCH PRESENTS:
TROPICAL SPELLS HOODOOS & VOODOOS

"The talisman and the ring (Figure No. 10) will make you invisible to all eyes, even those of the spirits. Only the Great Being could be witness to your steps and your actions. You will penetrate everywhere into the bosom of the seas, into the bowels of the earth, you can likewise survey the airs, and no action of men can be hidden from you. Say only: *Benatir, Cararkau, Dedos, Etinarmi.*"

I repeated these four words, and through the walls of the Pyramid I saw two Arabs who were on the plain and who were profiting by the obscurity to ransack a tomb where they hoped to find something of value.

"You will be able, when you wish, to prove the other things which I will have taught you, it will only be necessary to place the ring successively on the different fingers of the right hand.

No. 10

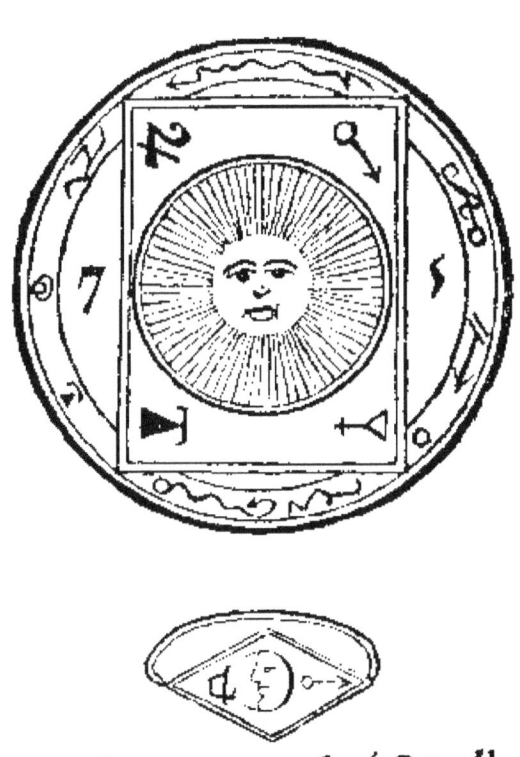

Characters to be engraved on the inside of the ring.

GYPSY WITCH PRESENTS:
TROPICAL SPELLS HOODOOS & VOODOOS

"The talisman and ring (Figure No. 11) will serve to transport you into whatever part of the world you judge appropriate without running any danger. Say merely these words: *Raditus, Polastrien, Terpandu, Ostrata, Pericatur, Ermas.* But I hope that you will not make use of these means to leave me without my consent. Promise it to me."

"My father, I swear to it."

No. 11

Characters to be engraved on the inside of the ring.

GYPSY WITCH PRESENTS:
TROPICAL SPELLS HOODOOS & VOODOOS

"With the talisman and the ring (Figure No. 12) you will be able to open all locks, no matter what secrets have been employed to shut them; you will not need a key. Simply by touching them with the ring and pronouncing these three words: *Saritap, Pernisox, Ottarim*, they will open of themselves without difficulty. Make proof of this on the spot, my son," the old man told me.

"Close the casket which you see on that table."

I did this, and after having assured myself that nothing could open it but the key, I touched it with the ring and pronounced the magic words, and it opened of its own accord.

"It will be the same," added the old man, "with all the doors of prisons where they might lock you up.

No. 12

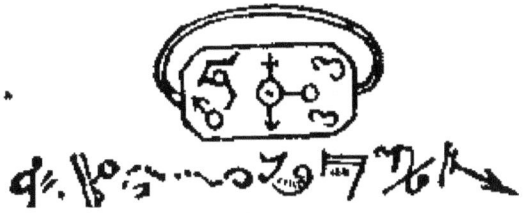

Characters to be engraved on the inside of the ring.

GYPSY WITCH PRESENTS:
TROPICAL SPELLS HOODOOS & VOODOOS

"With the talisman and ring (Figure No. 13), you will be able to see what takes place in all houses without being obliged to enter them; you will be able to read the thoughts of everyone whom you approach and with whom you find yourself, and you will be able to render them service or do them injury as you wish. It will be sufficient to place the talisman on your head and then to blow on the ring saying: *o Tarot, Nizael, Estarnas, Tantarez*, these words are for knowing the thoughts of people.

"In order to render service to those who deserve it, you say: *Nista, Saper, Visnos*, and they will immediately enjoy all sorts of prosperities. To punish the wicked and your enemies, you will say: *Xatros, Nifer, Roxas, Rortos*, and they will at once suffer punishment and frightful torment. What you have already seen should prove to you that I have advanced nothing which cannot be realized; therefore it is useless to make proof thereof.

No. 13

Characters to be engraved on the inside of the ring.

GYPSY WITCH PRESENTS:
TROPICAL SPELLS HOODOOS & VOODOOS

"The talisman and the ring (Figure No. 14) will serve you to destroy all the projects which could be made against you, and if any spirit wished to oppose your wishes, you could force him to submit to you. Place the talisman on a table under your left hand and with the ring on the second finger of the right hand, you say in a bass voice, while inclining your head: *Senapos, Terfita, Estamos, Perfiter, Notarin.*

Characters to be engraved on the inside of the ring.

GYPSY WITCH PRESENTS:
TROPICAL SPELLS HOODOOS & VOODOOS

"The talisman and ring (Figure No. 15) have a property as extraordinary as agreeable; they will give you all the virtues, all the talents, and the inclination to do good by changing all substances which are of a bad quality and rendering them excellent. For the first object, while elevating the talisman and with the ring placed on the first joint of the third finger of the left hand, it is sufficient to pronounce these words: *Turan, Estonos, Fuza*. For the second operation you say: *Vazotas, Testanar*, and you will see operate the wonder which I have proclaimed to you.

No. 15

Characters to be engraved on the inside of the ring.

GYPSY WITCH PRESENTS:
TROPICAL SPELLS HOODOOS & VOODOOS

"The talisman and the ring (Figure No. 16) will assist you to know all the minerals and vegetables, their virtues and properties, and you will possess the universal medicine. There is no illness that you will not be able to cure and no cure that you will undertake without success. Aesculapius and Hippocrates will only be novices compared to you. You pronounce only these words: *Reterrem, Salibat, Cratares, Hisater*, and when you are near a sick person you will carry the talisman on the stomach and the ring with a St. Andrew's Cross around your neck on a ribbon the color of fire.

No. 16

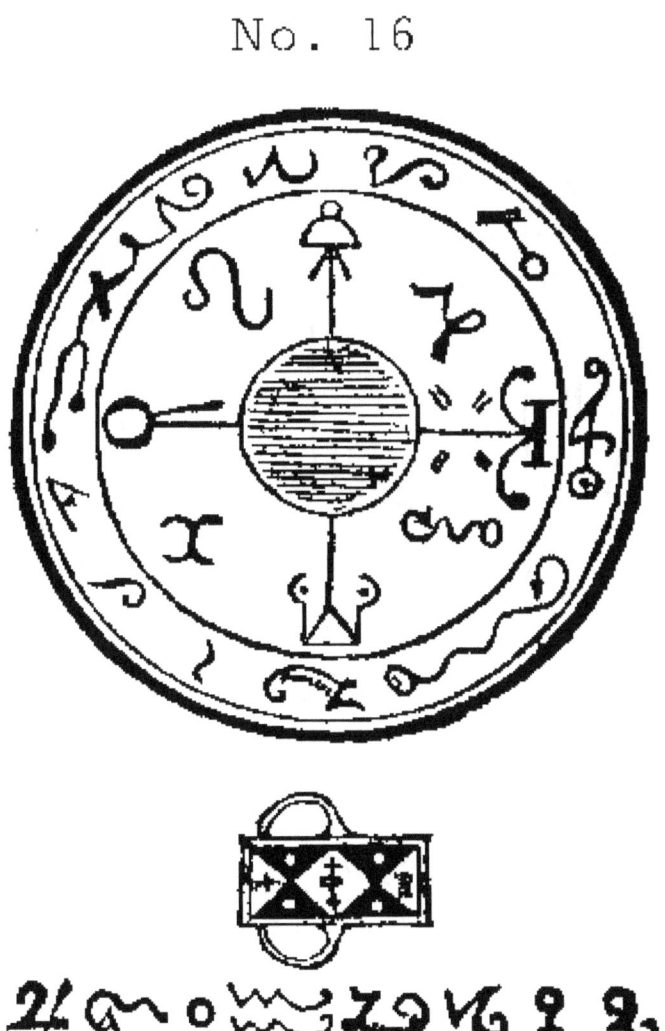

Characters to be engraved on the inside of the ring.

GYPSY WITCH PRESENTS:
TROPICAL SPELLS HOODOOS & VOODOOS

"The talisman and the ring (Figure No. 17) will keep you safe in the midst of the most ferocious animals, to subdue them to your will, to know by their different cries what they want as they have a language among themselves. Mad animals will keep at a distance from you, and you will make them perish forthwith by pronouncing the words which I am going to indicate to you. For the first operation it is sufficient to say: *Hocatos, Imorad, Surater, Markila.* For the second: *Trumantrem, Ricona, Estupit, Oxa.*

No. 17

Characters to be engraved on the inside of the ring.

GYPSY WITCH PRESENTS:
TROPICAL SPELLS HOODOOS & VOODOOS

"The talisman and ring (Figure No. 18) will enable you to know the good or bad intentions of all the individuals whom you will meet to guarantee you of it and to impress on their face a mark which will be noticed by everyone. It is sufficient to pronounce these mysterious words, while placing the talisman on your heart and the ring on the little finger of your right hand. You will then say: *Crostes, Furinot, Katipa, Garinos.*

Characters to be engraved on the inside of the ring.

GYPSY WITCH PRESENTS:
TROPICAL SPELLS HOODOOS & VOODOOS

"The talisman and the ring (Figure No. 19) will give you all talents and a profound understanding of all the arts so that you can perform with as much brilliance as the greatest masters and foremost artists. It is sufficient to carry the talisman and the ring in a manner you judge suitable while pronouncing these seven words: *Ritas, Onalun, Tersorit, Ombas, Serpitas, Quitathar, Zamarath*, while adding afterwards the name of the art or the talent which you wish to possess.

GYPSY WITCH PRESENTS:
TROPICAL SPELLS HOODOOS & VOODOOS

"The talisman and the ring (Figure No. 20) will help you to win at lotteries and to make certain when playing a game that you will obtain the fortune of your adversaries. You will place the talisman on your left arm, adjusting it with a white ribbon and the ring on the little finger of your right hand; then you will say these words: *Rokes*, for a selection, *Pilatus*, for a combination of two numbers, *Zotas*, for dice, *Tulitas*, for four winning numbers, *Xatanitos*, for five winning numbers. Be sure to pronounce all the words when you are on a quine and for a card game you will pronounce them each time the cards are shuffled, if it is you or your partner, and before commencing you will touch your left arm on the spot where the talisman is to be found with your right hand, and you will kiss your ring. All this must be done without drawing the attention of your adversary.

Characters to be engraved on the inside of the ring.

GYPSY WITCH PRESENTS:
TROPICAL SPELLS HOODOOS & VOODOOS

"The talisman and the ring (Figure No. 21) will enable you to direct all the infernal powers against your enemies or against those who would injure your friends. You will carry it in a manner which you consider suitable and pronounce merely these three words: *Osthariman, Visantiparos, Noctatur.*

No. 21

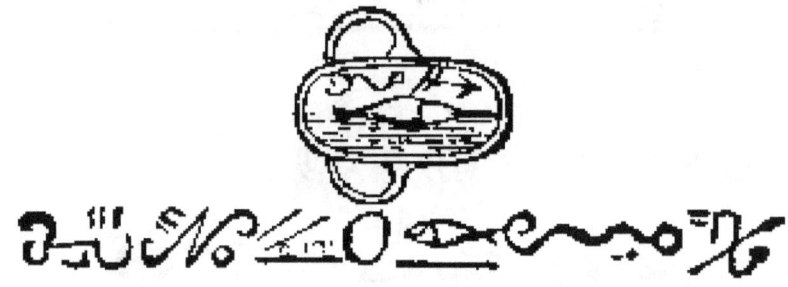

GYPSY WITCH PRESENTS:
TROPICAL SPELLS HOODOOS & VOODOOS

"The talisman and the ring (Figure No. 22) will serve you to recognize what the infernal powers wish to undertake, and you can abort all their projects by placing the talisman on your chest and the ring on the first joint of the little finger of the left hand. You pronounce these words: *Actatos, Catipta, Bejouran, Itapan, Marnutus.*

No. 22

Characters to be engraved on the inside of the ring.

GYPSY WITCH PRESENTS: TROPICAL SPELLS HOODOOS & VOODOOS

COMPOSITION OF THE TALISMANS AND THE RINGS

"As it is possible that you have not had the means of making talismans and rings similar to mine," the old man said to me, "you will make them up in the manner which I will indicate. Know that the rings are of bronzed steel with the characters engraved thereon. The talismans should be made of silk cloth in the dimensions of the figures.

No. 1. White satin embroidered in gold.

No. 2. Red satin embroidered in silver.

No. 3. Sky-blue satin embroidered in silver.

No. 4. Black satin embroidered in silver.

No. 5. Green satin embroidered in gold.

No. 6. Violet satin embroidered in silver.

No. 7. Golden-yellow satin embroidered in gold.

No. 8. Lilac satin with shaded silk.

No. 9. Poppy-red satin embroidered in silver.

No. 10. Yellow satin embroidered in black silk.

No. 11. Puce satin embroidered in gold.

No. 12. Dark blue satin embroidered in silver.

No. 13. Pale grey satin embroidered in gold.

No. 14. Rose satin embroidered in silver.

No. 15. Golden-yellow satin embroidered in silver.

GYPSY WITCH PRESENTS:
TROPICAL SPELLS HOODOOS & VOODOOS

No. 16. Orange satin embroidered in silver.

No. 17. Dark green satin embroidered in gold.

No. 18. Black satin embroidered in gold.

No. 19. White satin embroidered in black silk.

No. 20. Cherry satin embroidered in silver.

No. 21. Grey-White satin, shaded.

No. 22. Red satin, embroidered in the middle with gold, the border in silver, and the signs in black and white silk.

The old man, after having given me this information, replaced all the talismans and rings in the casket. The spirit who was at my side closed it arid gave him the key. The old man said to me: "All the wonders which have been performed in front of you, my dear son, ought not to leave any doubt of the Power and virtue of these talismans and rings. If you have not experienced any obstacle in your enterprises, it is because your heart is pure, that your soul is without stain, and that virtue, probity, and honor will always be dear to you. A man who had the least reproach to make to himself, who had destroyed the good of others, or who had only the intention of so doing, would not be able to participate in our mysteries. In vain would he have in his possession all that you see, our magical language known to him. The celestial powers—aerial, infernal, terrestrial, and those of the oceans and fire—would rebel against him. All that he wished to undertake would turn to his shame and his confusion, and at each invocation which he might make, the powers that he implored for help and intervention would answer him: Renounce thy projects. Thou art guilty. Before commanding us, purify thyself, expiate thy faults.

"If after these emanations he continued to conjure the powers, he would finish by being punished and would without fail lose his life. Remember then, my dear son, that all is possible with virtue and that not one fault will remain unpunished. There are still two prayers which you must be careful to recite before and after each conjuration that you wish to do; here they are:

GYPSY WITCH PRESENTS: TROPICAL SPELLS HOODOOS & VOODOOS

FIRST PRAYER

The Celestial Fire above is an incorruptible flame, always scintillating, the source of life, fountain of all the Beings, and principle of all things. This flame produces all and nothing perishes except which it consumes: it makes itself known by it-self. This fire cannot be contained in any place; it is without body or matter. It encompasses the skies, and from it emanates a little spark which makes all fire of the Sun, of the Moon, and the Stars. That is what I know of God: do not try to know more because that is beyond you, such judge as thou art. Moreover, know that the unjust or wicked man can-not hide himself in front of God; no address or any excuse can disguise anything from his piercing eyes. All is clear to God: God is everywhere.

SECOND PRAYER

There is in God as immense profundity of flame; the heart ought not, however, to fear to touch or to be touched by this adorable fire; it will not be consumed by this sweet fire, whose tranquil and perishable heat makes the union, harmony, and duration of the world. Nothing exists except by this fire which is God. No one has engendered it; it is without mother, it knows all, and no one is able to know anything of it. It is immovable in its projects and its name is ineffable. Here then is that which is God; because for us, who are his messengers, we are but a small part of God.

"You see, my son, that all the instructions that I give you have as a basis the respect which one owes to God, Who is the principle of all things and whose ineffable and limitless goodness fills us to the brim each day with all His goodness, when we render ourselves worthy of it by our respect and our submission to His will and His immutable decree."

THE BLACK HEN

The old man after these short reflections said to me: "You have no doubt noticed, my son, that I have spoken to you about the birds to whom I was going to give food, and you have seen spirits who had one with them; when the pieces of gold were deposited at your

GYPSY WITCH PRESENTS:
TROPICAL SPELLS HOODOOS & VOODOOS

feet, it was these birds who enabled them to discover it by their instinct and by the magical and cabalistic words which one pronounced. To procure these birds there are difficulties without number that one must conquer, and the profane, those who are not initiated into our mysteries, make useless efforts to obtain them. It is of the marvelous Black Hen that I am going to converse with you. The great Oromasis, father of Zoroaster, was the first who possessed one; it is from him that I possess the secret of calling them into existence, and here is the manuscript in which is contained the manner of hatching these birds who are as rare as precious."

He opened for me at the same time this manuscript whose cover was a thin plate of gold covered with diamonds, rubies, topazes and sapphires whose brilliance it was impossible to bear. The paper was of a dazzling whiteness, and the hieroglyphic characters were traced by hand in rose-colored ink.

"I will teach YOU to read in this book as I can," he said to me, "but let us occupy ourselves with the way to hatch the Black Hen and to procure the eggs which she will come forth."

He took several pieces of aromatic woods such as aloes, cedar, or lemon, laurel, some root of Iris, and some roses whose leaves had been dried in the sun. (Translators note: the author distinctly states leaves, not petals.)

He put the lot in a chafing-dish of gold, poured on top thereof balsamic oil of the purest essence, transparent gum, and having pronounced the words: *Athas, Solinam, Erminatos, Pasaim*, the sun-light penetrated the vault.

He placed a glass on the chafing-dish. At the same moment that the sun's struck the glass, the perfumes and pieces of odorous wood which were in the dish burst into flame, the glass liquefied, and an agreeable odor was diffused in the vault. Very soon nothing was left but cinders.

The old man, who had not ceased to watch with the greatest attention, took a golden egg which been in a black velvet bag and which I had not noticed. He opened this egg, closed the burning cinders therein, and placed it then on a black cushion.

He covered it with a faceted rock-crystal bell; then, raising his eyes and his arms toward the vault, he cried: *o Sanataper, Ismai, Nontapilus, Ertivaler, Canopistus*. The sun seemed to dart its rays on this bell with still greater force and violence.

The bell became the color of fire, the golden egg disappeared before my eyes, a thin vapor rose in the air, and I saw a little black pullet which stirred, got to its feet and clucked

GYPSY WITCH PRESENTS:
TROPICAL SPELLS HOODOOS & VOODOOS

faintly. The old man extended one of his fingers to it, and it placed itself thereon. He then pronounced these two words: *Binusas, Testipas*, and the winged creature glided onto his breast.

"There," said the old man, "is the manner of procuring a Black Hen. In a few days it will be of ordinary size, and I will instruct it in front of you. You will see the instinct of this animal to discover the most hidden treasures and that the smallest particle of gold cannot escape it. Let us give thanks to the Great Being who has permitted us to penetrate these mysteries and to perform such prodigies and marvels. We will say together the two prayers recounted further back."

After having fulfilled this duty, he said to me, "My son, this is enough. We will take a little rest."

The sun had shone on us for some time. It disappeared, and its light was replaced by that of several chandeliers. The spirit, who had not left us, took a lyre, and accompanying himself he sang in the language of the magicians of the Eternal Power and the marvels of nature.

The old man listened with attention to the accents of the spirit. For myself I was enchanted, arid he smiled in observing me.

"This is enough," he said to the spirit.

"Before delivering ourselves to rest, I wish to show you the means of having a Black Hen without having recourse to those which I have used, for it would be difficult to obtain the perfumes and the other materials which I placed in the chaffing-dish if others than you or I wished to perform this great work. But if someday you find someone who is worthy of being initiated, here is the means which you should employ. Take an egg which you will expose at noon to the gleams of the sun, observing that it has not the least stain. Then you choose a hen as black as possible; if it has any feathers of another color, you will pull them out. You will cover its head with a hood of black material in such a manner that it can-not distinguish anything. You will allow it the use of its beak. Enclose it in a box lined also with black material, big enough to contain it, and place that in a room where daylight cannot penetrate. Be careful to bring it food only at night. When all these indispensable precautions have been taken, you will give it the egg to sit on, taking care that it is not disturbed by any noise. It all depends on the blackness of this hen, its imagination will be impressed with it, and at the proper time you will see hatched a hen which is completely black. But I repeat to you, is necessary that those who perform this shall be worthy by their wisdom and virtue to participate in these sacred and divine mysteries. For, if we

GYPSY WITCH PRESENTS: TROPICAL SPELLS HOODOOS & VOODOOS

are not able to read the hearts of men, it is not the same with the Great Spirit; all is known to him and he penetrates our most secret intentions and our most hidden thoughts. It is after that that He accords or refuses to us His favors and His gifts.

"Our sitting has been so long," he added, "that we must take some food before delivering ourselves to rest."

He clapped his hands three times, and the Slaves, the spirits who had previously appeared, offered themselves again to my attention, and in an instant we had all the viands that could satisfy taste aroma, and the eyes. The meal was very gay; the old man animated it by his sallies. The spirit was also of the party. I was as inspired, and I joined the conversation. At last sleep weighed down our eyes, and we left the table to taste its sweetness.

The most agreeable dreams lulled me with their cheerful images, and when I awoke daylight lit up our abode. I did not see the old man or the spirit. I thought that they had gone out, and I abandoned myself to my reflections. The present assures me of the future, nothing could make me anxious. If fortune gives happiness, I said to myself, who will be happier than I. I cannot see any wish which will not be accomplished at once; my lot would be envied if it were known by the remainder of men. I want to be able to return to my country soon.

As I followed up this idea, I heard a slight noise and saw the old man enter followed by the spirit. They approached me, both took me by the hand, and I left my bed of rest at once.

"You have rested well, my dear son," the old man said.

"During your sleep I went out with the spirit to visit my birds, and I am going to make you acquainted with their talents. At the same instant he touched a spring which was in the wall, a section opened, and seven black birds which I recognized as hens were brought in a cage by two black slaves.

"These animals have a marvelous instinct for finding gold. You will be the judge."

He placed several pieces of gold under the cushions, in the crevices of walls under the folds of his turban, and then said to the slaves: *Tournabos, Fativos, Almabisos.* They opened the cage, uncovered the heads of the birds, and the hens came out and flew immediately in the different places where the gold was hidden. They picked up the pieces in their beaks and deposited them at the feet of the old man. He took these birds one after the other and caressed them.

He said to me: "You see how tame they are; we will go out for a while on the plain; I have placed in the sand several pieces

GYPSY WITCH PRESENTS:
TROPICAL SPELLS HOODOOS & VOODOOS

of gold. We will release our birds, and soon they will have discovered the treasure." He made a sign to the slaves who placed the birds back in the cage and we departed.

As soon as we had come out of the Pyramid for about five hundred paces onto the plain, he released the birds. They went a few paces; soon it seemed that their instinct indicated to them where the treasure was to be found. They flew in that direction, and all seven of them started scratching. They soon discovered the sacks, and one of them started to cackle; we approached and saw the sacks which the old man had hidden. I could not prevent myself from showing my surprise.

"My son, you see that all is possible with the aid of God and his powerful protection."

We took the sacks and reentered the Pyramid. He had the birds re-enclosed with the same precautions as were taken to let them out. He then said to me: "Let us see what condition my newborn is in."

He opened a little box lined with down in which he had enclosed it, and already feathers were beginning to appear.

"A few more days," he said, "and it will be able to receive the first lessons. He replaced the box in its place.

"Since we have been together," said the old man, "we have not gone out; we will make a little excursion into the country and wear the costume of the locality."

The spirit covered his head with a turban and dressed completely like a Turk. I did the same, and we prepared to depart. Before leaving I saw the old man take a talisman and a ring. I remarked on it, and he told me that perhaps it might be necessary for us and that precaution was the mother of security. We then went our way and walked quietly for some time.

The old man spoke to us of the changes which took place in the world from time to time, of the revolution of the stars and the planets. He seemed to give notice to us and to foreshadow things which would follow.

All of a sudden a horde of Arabs pounced upon us with raised swords. The old man looked at them without fright, and he raised his hand; the brigands stopped. He pronounced the words prescribed for the talisman (Figure No. 10) and we became invisible. The astonished Arabs looked on all sides without seeing us. It is impossible to paint a picture of the astonishment of these villains. Their chief appeared astounded. The old man smiled. He pronounced the word *Natarter* in a loud voice, and they took flight with lightening rapidity.

GYPSY WITCH PRESENTS: TROPICAL SPELLS HOODOOS & VOODOOS

"Be calm," said the old man. "For a long time they will not dare to appear in this territory."

We continued walking for some time. The time passed with an extraordinary rapidity; the conversation of the old man was so varied, so instructive, that it was impossible to listen to him without being charmed by all that he said.

"Let us return to our abode." After having pronounced these words, he looked at the sun and cried: "Brilliant star, image of the Divinity, thou who vivifies the earth and gives life to nature, receive my homage; may I ere I leave the Earth constantly enjoy thy light."

"What has given birth to these somber ideas," I immediately cried. "Why do you think of leaving Earth?"

"Ah, my son! Each day which passes, each that we take leads us towards the tomb. Lucky is the just man who can go to sleep in peace in the care of God to enjoy thereafter the rewards promised to virtue. Also, my son, do you believe that I do not concern myself with my last hour? At my age it is permitted to think of it, and I have always lived in a manner so as to be able to die without fear. I am 270 years old, and I have seen many things pass; I will pass also when my turn comes. And now enough of this matter. I see that I trouble you, and that is not my intention. Let us talk of other things."

AN INFALLIBLE CALCULATION TO WIN LOTTERIES

"The talisman and ring (Figure No. 20) will furnish you with the means to win at lotteries. I wish also to indicate to you an infallible calculation to obtain the same advantages. It is really very simple. You take a game of piquet composed of thirty-two cards. You shuffle them, cut and extract nineteen cards one after the other commencing with that which is underneath. Take their numbers: know, the ace is 11, the king 4, the queen 3, the knave 2, and the other cards their numerical value. Add up the total. Then add the 30 or 31 days of the month in which you find yourself, your age, the day of your birth, that is to say, the first, second or third or such other day, and a date when you have proved something happy or agreeable: you add all these numbers, you take a third of it, and you place in the lottery the numbers which this addition has given you. You can be certain that these numbers will come out in totality or in part on the different wheels. For instance, if you find the numbers 13, 52, 73, you can take again 31, 25, 37, and the unities.

"This calculation is infallible. You can convince yourself. The

GYPSY WITCH PRESENTS:
TROPICAL SPELLS HOODOOS & VOODOOS

number 30 is privileged, and it is from this that all is calculated for 3 times 30 makes 90; it is from this that one does not wish to exceed this number in the lottery. It is the same with all games.

"The numbers which have 3 for a root are the most fortunate; odd is all. God, after having created the world and being occupied for six days in establishing the admirable order which exists, rested on the seventh, which is odd. Let us take God as an example and a model in all that we do and we will be assured in all that we undertake. You have noticed, my son, that odd numbers are the basis of all the mysterious operations into which I have initiated you."

We continued our route and arrived at the Pyramid. He opened the door, and we went down. Arriving in the hall, we sat down on a sofa which faced the table on which was the casket of the talismans. The old man replaced the one which had served to clear away the Arabs, and we remained in silence for some time.

The old man appeared tired. He reclined on the and soon he was asleep. I cast my eyes on his venerable figure, and I admired his serenity, Calmness spread over all his features. I remarked about this to the spirit who told me: "It is the image of his soul. I have obeyed him for more than a century. You cannot have any idea of his virtue, of his wisdom, of his goodness. His days are numerous, and all are marked by some good deed, of the unhappy he has rescued without their ever knowing who the being was who came to their help. If the eternal Soul who has created all should take the figure of a mortal, it is his which He would borrow. Is not the just man in effect the image of God on earth? Many have taken title, but how many have usurped it and merited little."

After having pronounced these words, the spirit got up, knelt on the ground near the old man, and raising his hands and eyes towards heaven, said in a solemn tone which awed me: "Eternal Spirit, Who hears me and Who reads heart, prolong the life of this virtuous man. Ensure that he adorns by his presence for a long time to come the earth which You enrich with Thy gifts, unless You have reserved for him near Thee a reward worthy of him."

The sentiments with which he expressed these words keenly moved me. Tears wet my eyes, and I fell on my knees as he had.

The old man awoke at this moment, and casting his eyes on us, he said to us with a smile, "What are you doing, my children?" I answered that we were praying to the Great Being to conserve our father for us.

"My good friends," answered the old man, "our life has a term set by Providence which we cannot extend. Everything begins,

GYPSY WITCH PRESENTS:
TROPICAL SPELLS HOODOOS & VOODOOS

everything must end; God alone is eternal. The only thing which can survive us is the memory of our virtues and the good examples which we have set. While like voyagers we can perceive the course of our destiny and what good or evil we have done as we have been more or less the slaves of our passions, happy is he who has been able to command himself and to distinguish the happiness which is praiseworthy from what is not. For myself, I have been happy enough; I made the distinction in the springtime of my life, and in the winter I taste the sweetness. I shall soon return into the bosom of Him who has created me; a dream announced it to me in my sleep. In a few hours my soul will leave its mortal remains and will rise towards the celestial regions."

"Oh heavens my father!" I cried, "What do you announce?"

"What you must await like myself, my dear son but I bless my departure since I have the consolation in dying of leaving my heritage to a man who is deserving, who loves virtue, who practices it, and who will never step aside from it. I will inform you of my last wishes, and you will execute them punctually if you love me and if you are grateful."

"Oh my father!" I cried, "Can you doubt it?"

"No, my dear son, I do not doubt at all. Now listen to me. All these treasures, all the jewels enclosed in this subterranean apartment, also the talismans and the rings, the slaves, and the birds which you have seen are yours. To you Odous," he said to the spirit, "I cannot do more than pronounce all my tenderness for one whom I have found worthy to succeed me. Love him, serve him as you would me, and from the Celestial Sphere to which I shall soon arise, I will watch over you."

He clapped his hands and all the slaves appeared.

"Here is your master," he said to them. "Be obedient to him, I order you."

They all came and prostrated themselves at my feet.

"Extend your hand over them as a sign of domination," the old man said to me.

I obeyed. They arose, and the old man's having made a sign, they disappeared. He added, "Take the gold urn which you will find in the cabinet on the right and place it on the table.

When I no longer exist, place my body in the middle of this chamber. Take the aromatic woods, which you will find near the coffers filled with gold, and surround me with them. After having poured over the pyre the liquid enclosed in the vase suspended from the roof, you will use the talisman with which I formed the egg in which was enclosed the Black Hen. After having pronounced

GYPSY WITCH PRESENTS:
TROPICAL SPELLS HOODOOS & VOODOOS

the mysterious words, you will set the funeral-pile on fire to consume my mortal remains. Take the ashes and enclose them in the urn. Conserve them. Men, cherish my memory; I die content. I would have liked to show you the means of instructing the little Black Pullet, but Heaven which knows our projects has not wished it so. Odous will teach you; he also knows this secret. I feel my soul ready to fly away. Come, my dear son, dry your tears so that I can press you once again to my heart. Remember, death is only dreaded by the guilty and the unjust man."

I approached him and he gave me a last kiss.

"Good-bye, my dear son," he said. "Listen to my last wishes."

While I was still bending over the sofa, he expired. I could not help myself saying, while sobbing, that the death of the just is sweet and worthy of envy. I fell almost unconscious at the feet of my benefactor.

Odous brought me back to my senses by observing that we had to obey our father. We then punctually performed that which he had ordered, and soon there remained only the ashes of the most just and most virtuous of men.

I said to Odous, "We will leave this day and make all the necessary arrangements for returning to my country."

"I am with you," answered the spirit. "Your wishes are law for me; command and I obey."

I had all the slaves brought before me and had them put on French costumes. It sufficed me to have recourse to the talismans. I had all the treasures and the effects which were in the underground vaults transported to the banks of the Nile and provided for the precious urn which I personally kept.

Odous found a boat and we went down the river. Very soon we entered the roadstead where a vessel was about to set sail for Marseilles. I boarded with all my people, and soon we were in mid-ocean. The captain of the vessel and the sailors examined us with extreme curiosity. As I spoke all languages at will, they were even more surprised.

Night came and the wind rose. The captain told me that he feared a storm. I told him that his vessel was good and would resist it. The tempest drew near, the sea became furious. Fear and despair were on all faces. The pilot could no longer control the ship. Only I, calm and tranquil, seemed unmoved.

Provided with the talisman and ring (Figure No. 9) and pronouncing the mysterious words, I seized the tiller and the vessel which, the instant before, was the plaything of the winds and the surrounding waves, sailed forward lightly over the vast bosom of

GYPSY WITCH PRESENTS: TROPICAL SPELLS HOODOOS & VOODOOS

the sea. The whole crew regarded me as a god, even giving me that name.

"I am but man," I told them. "My friends, I do not frighten easily, I know the art of navigation, and you see, it is only necessary to be composed to stand the storm at bay."

The rest of our voyage was very happy. We arrived at Marseilles, and we passed through quarantine before stepping ashore. I paid for my passage and that of my followers with a generosity which astonished the captain. I gave a present to each man of the crew, and I departed crowned with their blessings.

I stayed for some time at Marseilles. Having written to the place of my birth, I found that my parents no longer were alive. They had died during my absence leaving me sole heir to their estates which I sold and the proceeds of which were sent to me.

I bought a lovely property on the outskirts of Marseilles, the beautiful sky of Provence pleasing me. I improved my house, and I had a delightful stay.

The riches I possessed were such that I could obtain at will all that I desired; even to place myself to my satisfaction. I had a few friends to whom I gave advice, who followed it, and who were all astonished at their prosperity. They were ignorant as to the source. I did not share my secrets with anyone.

Inclination has made me write this little volume. If those who procure it know how to profit from it and are worthy of penetrating the mysteries and the secrets it contains, they will gamble with luck reserved for virtue and wisdom. They must not become discouraged. Constant and stubborn work will surmount everything says an ancient proverb.

They should thus work, and if success does not crown their efforts, they must lay the blame on themselves. It is because they are not pure and virtuous. The incredulous, the ignorant, and many others whom it is useless to designate will treat me as a fool, a visionary, an importunist. It matters little to me. The truth is there. I do not seek to repel injuries, still less censure. Certain family libraries, which have no other merit than to get hold of what belongs to others, will perhaps make haste to publish a surreptitious edition of this work. This is the only thing which I will punish with a talisman which I am keeping to myself and a ring more curious still.

I reserve for myself the decoration the perpetrator with two ears six inches longer than those provided of yore for King Midas who had been well judged. It is a warning which I give in passing to certain editors. You notice that for a sorcerer I do not push my

GYPSY WITCH PRESENTS:
TROPICAL SPELLS HOODOOS & VOODOOS

vengeance very far. And you, for whom I have written this work, you who seek to enlighten yourself, to penetrate, to understand the mysteries and the secrets of nature, work with consistency, persevere, and purify yourself to obtain success, the object of your wishes and your desires. Consider that the smallest stain with which your heart and your soul will be contaminated will be an invincible obstacle against success.

You will see the harbor without being able to enter and will be shipwrecked at the moment when you believe yourself saved. Watch, pray, hope. Adieu my dear and well loved readers. May you be able to play with all the ease which has become my lot. Amen.

The old man did not indicate to me the method of instructing the Black Pullet which he had hatched, but before expiring, he informed me that Odous would impart the important secret to me. When we were installed in my home in Marseilles, I reminded him of the old man's promise.

The Hen was of ordinary size and was eager to satisfy me. It had become so familiar that it hardly ever left me. I took particular care of it during our voyage, and if I have not mentioned this fact, it is because I judged it of little importance. We therefore occupied ourselves with the education of our bird. We placed a piece of gold in the basket where it was in the habit of sleeping and covered its eyes with the hood of which I have already spoken. Two or three days after that preliminary operation, each morning when I took it food to eat, it scratched in its basket, and taking the piece of gold in its beak, it guarded it until I took it.

One can see that the instinct of this bird was as extraordinary as marvelous. Odous said to me, "I have never yet seen as intelligent a one, but also, it is necessary to admit that our good and respected father employed a means to give it birth which was known only to himself and which he had never put into operation in front of me. This proves the tenderness and friendship he had given you. It will be necessary as from tomorrow to hide a piece of gold in the garden. We will carry our Hen to some distance, and we will see if she discovers it."

The next morning we did as agreed. I uncovered the head of my bird; it stayed on my knees for some time, looking in different directions. Finally, it jumped lightly to the ground and ran to the foot of a big tree where it started to scratch animatedly.

Odous said to me: "I guarantee that there is some treasure hidden at the foot of that tree. Let the Hen carry on."

She scratched all the time and to shorten the operation, I took

GYPSY WITCH PRESENTS:
TROPICAL SPELLS HOODOOS & VOODOOS

a spade which the gardener had left nearby, and after having scooped out about two feet, I discovered a case about four feet square and surrounded with iron bands. As we did not have the key, I sent Odous to find the talisman (Figure No. 12). He returned promptly and hardly had I attacked the lock with the ring than it opened, and we discovered several sacks filled with gold and silver, plate, diamonds, jewels, and several other precious objects which were valued at 1,500,000 francs. It seemed that these riches had been concealed in this place during the time of the civil troubles, and as the owners died without revealing their secret, nobody had any knowledge of this deposit.

I had bought this property from distant relatives. I could not prevent myself, nor could Odous, from admiring the instinct of our Black Hen, but it was equally necessary for it to find the other piece of hidden gold. We advanced a few steps, and she followed us. Soon she went ahead of us and stopped near the place where the gold was hidden. She soon found it and taking it in her beak, she deposited it at my feet.

"Charming bird," I cried! "How precious you are to me. You have put me in the place of a better man, the most tender and respected of fathers to me."

Odous said to me: "See if she will listen to the sacred words which must be pronounced every day to the Black Hen to indicate to her that she must look for things."

He then articulated certain words, *Nozos, Taraim, Ostus*. The Hen appeared to pay attention and to understand because she started to scratch near us and found a ruby mounted in a golden ring.

"I am going to pronounce three other words which should indicate to her that she should repose near her master."

He then said: *Seras, Coristan, Abattuzas*. The Hen came and placed herself at my feet.

Odous added: "All the hens which you possess know these words but it has taken some time to teach them. One must hold them with a ribbon: when pronouncing the first words, one must make them walk; when pronouncing the second, one stops them. As these birds are endowed with a particular instinct, they then do that which one desires."

Having the casket brought in by my slaves, I added the Pullet's findings to those which I already possessed.

I had an elegant pavilion constructed of Cremona marble, and I placed the urn containing the ashes of the old man on a black marble pedestal with a silver plaque which expressed my recognition and regrets. I had cypresses and weeping willows planted, and every day at the rising of the sun; I went, followed by Odous, to visit this pavilion and to pass an hour in support of our good father, remembering the lessons and examples of virtue which he had given me. I will cite several events with great solemnity: that on which he saved my life by taking me into the Pyramid and the anniversary of his death.

This day was consecrated to grief and meditation in my house. And once every year all my slaves entered the grove which I had had surrounded with a metal grill so that nobody could enter. Also, the thickness of the bushes and the winding paths which had to be wandered through before arriving at the pavilion prevented the most piercing eye from seeing it.

My days passed between work, study, meditation, and walking exercise. I received a few visitors in my home, but nobody had an inkling of that which passed in my private life. To live happily, live concealed, as a Sage said. And this proverb is the rule and foundation of my conduct.

GYPSY WITCH PRESENTS:
TROPICAL SPELLS HOODOOS & VOODOOS

From Hoodoo Curio Catalog, King Novelty Co. 1944

GYPSY WITCH PRESENTS:
TROPICAL SPELLS HOODOOS & VOODOOS

PART TWO
What is Hoodoo?

Hoodoo is considered to be folk magick which originated in the Caribbean islands and the southern United States. In addition, it draws significantly from Native American practices, especially in its use of herbs and other natural ingredients. The ultimate goal of hoodoo, as with any form of magick, is to allow people access to supernatural forces to influence their daily lives.

Hoodoo, also known as Rootwork or Conjure, is believed to act in many areas, including gambling, love, divination, cursing one's enemies, removing curses, and the treatment of sickness. Hoodoo is well known for its use of various homemade potions, charms, and candle magick, but there are also many successful commercial companies selling various hoodoo products.

Most hoodoo practitioners say that hoodoo is based on Christianity. The Bible, especially the Old Testament, is considered a powerful artifact in hoodoo. The Psalms and other passages are often read aloud as a part of spells, and the Bible itself can be a powerful talisman, particularly for protection and the healing of certain ailments.

With hoodoo, the Bible and biblical figures are reconceived according to supernatural and magical ideas; God is the greatest conjurer of all, using magick to create the world in six days.

European and European-American grimoires, such as *The Black Pullet*, also had an influence on the development of hoodoo. These spells, prayers and verses, along with herbs, roots, and curios are what make up hoodoo.

Despite what has been written by some ignorant historians, hoodoo is not Voodoo (Vodoun). Voodoo is a religion based on African religions brought over by slaves forced to work in the sugarcane fields on island in the Caribbean. With hoodoo, teachings and rituals are handed down from a one practitioner to another, but there are no priests or priestesses. There is some debate, but the name hoodoo may have been taken from the word Voodoo by outsiders who were looking for an overall name for

GYPSY WITCH PRESENTS: TROPICAL SPELLS HOODOOS & VOODOOS

rootworkers and conjurers, but other than that, the connections between the two are strictly superficial.

FOLK MAGICK AND TROPICAL SPELLS

Hoodoo is a way to use the mysterious forces of the universe to try and obtain a need or desire. At various times in our lives, we are frustrated in our attempts to achieve a goal. It is simply the way life is that we cannot have everything that we desire. However, since the beginning of time, people have sought other ways to try and fulfill their wants and needs. Thus was created folk magick, the first branch of what would later grow and develop into hoodoo.

Folk magic was born in an age of mystery. Thousands of years ago, nature was a strange force, points of light hung far overhead in the sky. Invisible forces ruffled hair and kicked up dust storms. Water fell from the sky. Powerful forces, inconceivable to humans, sent flashes of light from the skies, blasting trees into ashes. Women miraculously bore young. All that lived eventually died. Blood was sacred, food was sacred. Water, the Earth, plants, animals, the wind and all that existed was infused with power.

Folk magick slowly developed from these beginnings. Every group, every tribe had its own forms of ritual. Folk magick differed from structured religion and organized magick, this was the realm of personal magic, performed for personal reasons. A woman dressed a wound with a plantain leaf that she had gathered with her left hand to increase its healing properties. The fisherman rubbed his bone hooks with flowers to attract fish. Love-sick teens gathered heart-shaped stones and presented these to the objects of their desire.

These simple rituals continued to be used for many thousands of years, particularly in isolated areas. With the growing tide of organized religions, many of the old ways of folk magick were forgotten. Others were altered to outwardly conform to the new religions. That magick which couldn't be made to at least vaguely conform to the new religion was practiced in secret.

However, folk magick had not died out completely, folk

GYPSY WITCH PRESENTS:
TROPICAL SPELLS HOODOOS & VOODOOS

magick continued to exist. Throughout the Far, Near and Middle East, in Africa, Polynesia and Australia, in Central and South America, in rural sections of North America such as the Ozarks, in Hawaii and even in parts of Europe, folk magick still existed and was practiced.

Hoodoo arose during the 19th century within the African-American community. Hoodoo was at first predominately practiced within the Southern states. However, as families relocated to northern cities, hoodoo became established all across the nation.

During the 1960's, folk magick saw a rebirth. The youth movement in the United States rebelled against rigid social codes and Christian ideals. Some young persons turned to Buddhism, Zen and other Eastern teachings. Others became entranced with what little they could learn of spells, charms, herb magic, tarot cards, amulets and talismans. Countless popular books and articles appeared, revealing this once public knowledge to a new generation dissatisfied with their purely technological lives.

Today, this resurgence has produced a generation of aware individuals. Many of these folk magicians have also become involved in channeling, psychic healing, herbal medicine, crystal consciousness, vegetarian diets, meditation and hoodoo. Folk magick constitutes the bulk of ancient and modern magickal techniques practiced by individuals to improve their lives.

What folk magick isn't is almost as important as what it is. It isn't the "Devil's work." It isn't "Satanism." It doesn't involve sacrifices of humans or animals. It isn't talking to spirits or calling up "demons." It isn't dark, dangerous or evil. Folk magick isn't anti-Christian or anti-religion. Folk magick can protect against evil forces. It is a tool with which people can transform their lives. When normal means fail, when all efforts have brought no results, many millions today turn to folk magick.

At the heart of folk magick is the spell. This is simply a ritual in which various tools are purposefully used, the goal is fully stated, and energy is moved to bring about the needed result. Spells are usually misunderstood by non-practitioners. In popular thought, all you need to perform magic is a spell.

GYPSY WITCH PRESENTS: TROPICAL SPELLS HOODOOS & VOODOOS

In folk magick, spells, words, chants, gestures with tools, are the outer form only. The real magick, the movement of energy, is within the magician. No demonic power flows to help the spell-caster. Instead, the magickian – by correctly performing a genuine spell, builds up the power within. At the proper time this power is released to work in manifesting the spell.

Effective spells are designed to facilitate this energy. So, while "true" spells do exist, the actual magick isn't in the words or tools, it is within the folk magician. Real spells are being written every day. Old spells have no more power than new ones.

Although personal power, that which resides within the magician, is the most potent force at work in folk magick, practitioners borrow freely from the spells and rituals of various cultures, using a wide variety of magical equipment. These tools are used to help focus the mental energies and put the magician in the proper frame of mind to perform the spell. Folk magick also affects the collective unconscious, removing the filters we put upon ourselves every day. However, no matter how many times the magick is performed, it will not work unless you support the magick with action. Magick works by using coincidence, so be alert when the conjunctions start to happen.

Folk magick spells can be as simple as reciting a short chant over a fresh rose while placing it between two pink candles in order to draw love; forming and retaining an image of the needed result in the mind; or placing the right ingredients into a Mojo bag for protection purposes. To perform effective magick three necessities must be present: The Need, the Emotion and the Knowledge.

HOODOO TOOLS

For those who practice hoodoo, (sometimes referred to as "two-headed-doctors") there is no limit of available tools that can be used. In the Sea Islands magickal medicines use animals parts like feathers, blood, and bones, human substances like hair clippings and fingernails, and other natural materials like leaves, sand, and water.

GYPSY WITCH PRESENTS: TROPICAL SPELLS HOODOOS & VOODOOS

In the United States, a conjurer can use herbs, plants, roots, trees, animals, magnets, minerals, and natural waters combined with magickal amulets, chants, ceremonies, rituals, and handmade power objects. These tools have been a part of hoodoo rootwork practice for as far back as oral histories and written records exist. It is very likely that their use combines African traditions of healing, Native American plant lore, and information derived from medieval European herbals, grimoires, and "books of wonders" such as those attributed to Albertus Magnus.

Some of the occult symbolism in the old herbals is based on the doctrine of signatures, where the shape, texture, or color of a plant is a sign of its mystic uses. Other magickal ascriptions are extensions of the ways that certain herbs are used in folk medicine. Thus violet leaves, which look like hearts, are worn in the shoe because they are alleged to attract a new lover, while angelica root, which contains phyto-estrogens and is a standard folk remedy for women's reproductive health problems, is carried in a conjure bag or woman's nation sack to protect mother and child from harm.

In addition to plants and herbs that can be gathered during a days walk in the woods, since the early 20th century conjurers have been able to buy a plethora of hoodoo-related items from various supply houses. These items could be found in certain stores, but hoodoo supplies were also available by mail order and through agents (people who sold products to friends and neighbors). As noted by Catherine Yronwode on the website Luckymojo.com, agents who sold these supplies were usually part-time beauticians as well as hoodoo rootworkers.

"They would come to your house to fix your hair (selling you the cosmetics and hair preparations they had bought wholesale) and they would also do psychic consultations and perform rootwork and conjuration, using the curios available from the same sources."

These agents carried their company's retail catalogs with them, and you could order candles, powders, formula oils, books, and other supplies that were mailed directly to your home.

Unfortunately, as urbanization has driven people farther

GYPSY WITCH PRESENTS:
TROPICAL SPELLS HOODOOS & VOODOOS

from the sources of natural magick in their lives, manufacturers of hoodoo products have slowly begun to leave the roots and herbs out of the old root doctors' formulas. Today, few companies sell hoodoo oils made with actual botanical ingredients.

According to Yronwode, hoodoo products, if they are made the old, traditional Southern way, should consist of more than just time-honored names. They should contain real herbs, roots, and minerals.

Magickal Talismans, also known as Amulets, Charms, or Lucky Pieces are small objects that are created or specially crafted to carry, draw, or amplify a specific quality of the person, such as strength or luck; to bring about a certain desired condition, such as sexual attractiveness or gambling wins; or to remove an unwanted condition, such as the negativity caused by jealous rivals or envious onlookers.

Talismans are an ancient magickal form, common in many cultures. They are frequently inscribed with signs, seals, sigils, or words, which may be written in magickal alphabets or in plain writing. The inscribed words or images may be in the form of a prayer to the Almighty, or they may invoke a specific spirit. They may also be in the form of a seal, as those from the *6th and 7th Book of Moses* or the *Seal of Solomon*.

Talismans, charms, and lucky pieces can be crafted or created to protect the bearer or bring luck to their owner. They are often made in the shape of a small object such as a coin or a small packet, and they may be carried in the pocket, worn as visible jewelry, carried as key chains, or hidden on the person. Common ways of carrying a hidden talisman include having the lucky or protective charm sewn into clothing, carried in the bosom, secreted in a compartment of a purse or wallet, or in the pocket of a pair of pants.

As was observed earlier with the manuscript *The Black Pullet*, many traditional hoodoo spiritual workers offer talismans whose imagery and intent are drawn from old-time Jewish sources like the *Key of Solomon* and the *6th and 7th Books of Moses*. Books describing such talismanic seals have been known among African-American root doctors since the late 19th century, and the amulets themselves, along with copies of the

GYPSY WITCH PRESENTS:
TROPICAL SPELLS HOODOOS & VOODOOS

seals printed on parchment paper, have been offered through mail order houses catering to conjurers and root doctors since the early 1900's

Solominic and Mosaic seals printed on parchment paper may be carried in small cloth or leather wallets or folded and inserted into mojo hands and conjure bags. Each seal has a specific usage, according to Jewish magickal traditions. For instance, a seal of Jupiter may be used for wealth, while a seal of the Sun may be used for the improvement ones health. Petitions, prayers, or portions of Biblical text may also be written on the back of the seals.

In addition to manmade amulets, there are natural curios that are employed as magickal talismans. Whole roots like John the Conqueror root are carried for male power and gambling luck; Queen Elizabeth root for female power and love luck; Nutmeg of India and Lucky Hand root, for gambling luck; Angelica root, for protection; and Master root, for domination and power over others.

Also highly prized are the lucky rabbit foot for good luck; the black cat bone to force a lover to return or for invisibility; and the alligator foot, for money-drawing.

Mineral talismans include lodestones, a single one for money-drawing and a matched pair for love-drawing; and pyrite, for luck with money and business.

Candles are also extremely popular in the use of hoodoo spells. They may be used for virtually any purpose, with the color and shape usually reflecting the type of spell being cast. Candles can be carved with appropriate symbols, loaded with personal items like hair or fingernail clippings, and anointed, dressed, or blessed with oils and herbs, roots, and minerals appropriate to the work. Sachet powders suitable to the spell can be dusted on it, or it may be sprinkled with glitter to reflect wishes out into the universe many times over.

Hoodoo oils, often called conjure oils, anointing oils, dressing oils, or condition oils, are made for practically any kind of circumstance. Authentic condition oils are made with natural ingredients, herbs, roots, and curios that have been added to a carrier oil and mixed with appropriate essential and in some cases fragrance oils.

Condition oils can be formulated to alleviate suffering, to

GYPSY WITCH PRESENTS:
TROPICAL SPELLS HOODOOS & VOODOOS

remove hindrances, or to draw specific changes and experiences to the client. Many of the old formula names clearly state the oil's purpose, like *Pay Me*, *Crown of Success*, and *Love Me*.

Hoodoo oils are used for anointing candles, mojo bags, talismans and enchanted jewelry, money, roots, and one's own body. They may be added to magical bags, jars, bottles, petitions, and amulets. Conjure oils are also used in the preparation of other common ingredients found in hoodoo like sachet powders, incense, and baths. They can be used to scent these preparations and also to determine the condition that they are focused on. The use of condition oils are in fact only limited by the imagination.

GYPSY WITCH PRESENTS:
TROPICAL SPELLS HOODOOS & VOODOOS

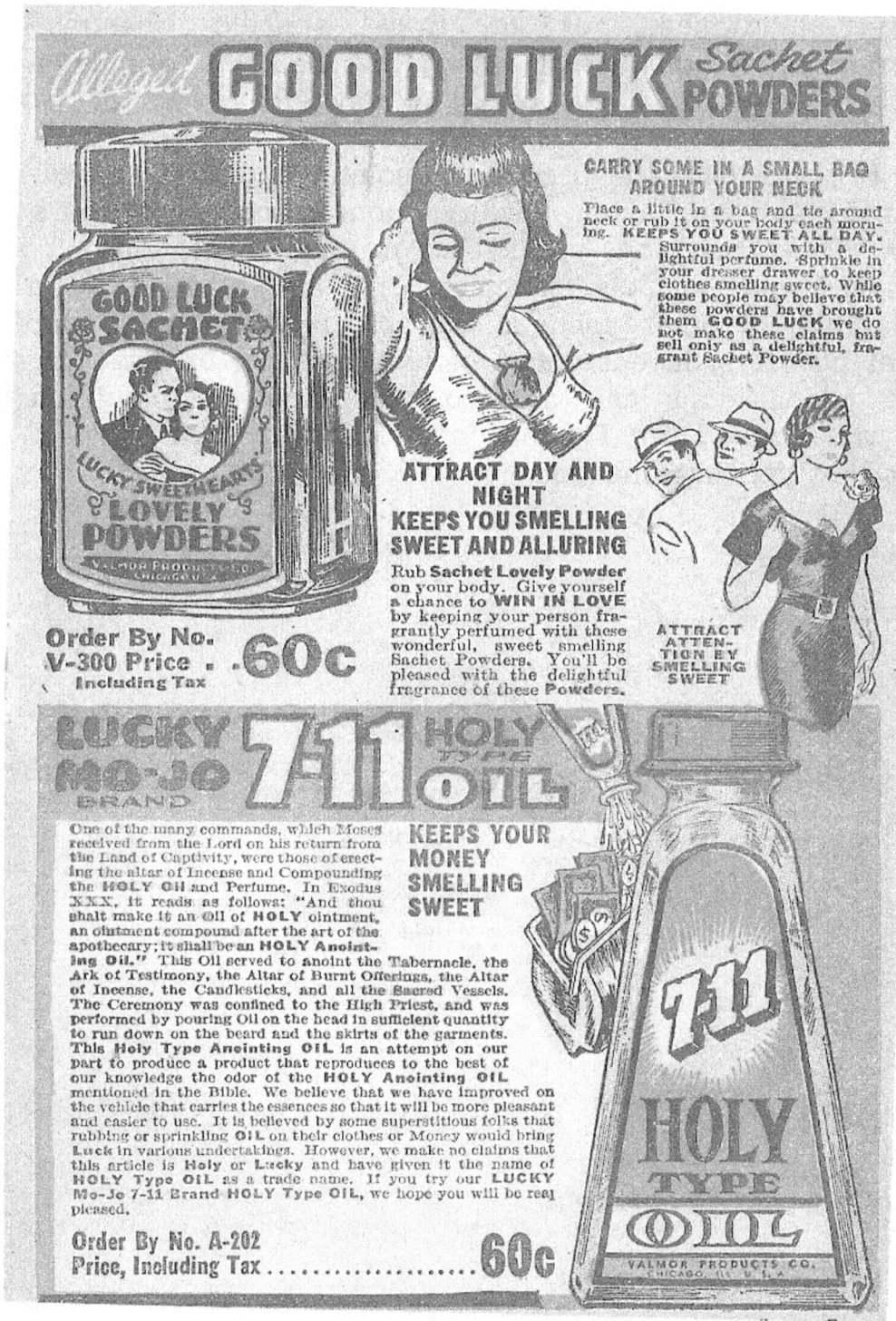

From Hoodoo Curio Catalog, King Novelty Co. 1944

GYPSY WITCH PRESENTS:
TROPICAL SPELLS HOODOOS & VOODOOS

PART THREE
Hoodoo Spells For Every Occasion

Cleansing and Protecting Ritual

Early in the morning, with the sunrise, take a lime, rub your whole body from top to bottom, or squeeze the juice and bathe in it. Then you go to the beach, walk backwards into the sea and dip yourself three times saying each time, "*In the name of the Lord.*" Your body and soul are once again clean and you will be protected from all harm for three days.

A Woman's Hand of Power

Into a black mojo bag add the following: One whole Angelica Root; One chunk of Dragons Blood Incense; One Piece of Frankincense; One Pinch of Myrrh; A bit of Gold leaf; One Oak Gall; One Piece of Mater Root; One Piece of Lightning Struck Wood; One Name Paper with your hairs in it folded towards you.

Feed it every Sunday with whiskey and it gives the woman that owns it strength of body and spirit.

A Man's Hand of Power

Into a black mojo bag add the following: One High John the Conqueror root; One piece of Sang Root (Ginseng Root); One chunk of Dragons Blood Incense; One Pinch of Myrrh; One chunk of Frankincense; A bit of Gold leaf; One Oak Gall; One piece of Master Root; One name paper folded towards you with one of your hairs in it.

Feed it with whiskey every Sunday and it will give the man that owns it strength of body and spirit.

GYPSY WITCH PRESENTS:
TROPICAL SPELLS HOODOOS & VOODOOS

Mojo Bag to Draw Prosperity

High John the Conqueror Root embodies the spirit of a heroic, fearless survivor of slavery. High John the Conqueror represents courage, strength, bravery, and the spirit of hope.

Begin this work on the waxing moon on a Thursday. Carefully select a High John the Conqueror Root that calls out to your spirit. Using your dominant hand (the most powerful hand) put root in a cup of sunflower oil. (Sunflowers possess positive energy because of their intimacy with Sun Ra). Stir in seven drops of Attar of Roses (substitute rose fragrance oil if necessary). Roses are soothing, healing plants that help us to receive blessings from the universe. Cap tightly. Swirl daily for fourteen days. Blot up any excess oil. Place fragrant High John, nutmeg, some cloves, and small cinnamon stick inside a four-by-six-inch piece of green flannel. Dip sewing needle in the sunflower and rose oil blend. Sew flannel together with green cotton thread. Feed bag at the beginning of the waxing moon and on full moon.

Food: sprinkle bag with a blend of powdered peppermint, lime, and basil (dried), magnetic sand, and sandalwood essential oil. You can also feed your money powdered High John root to draw prosperity or sprinkle it with basil.

Bottle Spell to Coerce Love

For this spell you will need: 9 pins, Black or Red candle, Restless Powder, 5 Senses Oil, Appropriate love oil to your case (Attraction, Come to Me, Return to Me, etc.), Bottle, No One But Me Powder, I Can You Can't Powder, Red Ants, Cinnamon (chip or stick). You will also need something personal from your target (hair, nail clippings etc.).

Begin by fixing the black candle by carving your target's name on it. Dress it with the love oil, 5 Senses oil, and Restless powder. Then stick into it 9 pins, evenly spaced and going

GYPSY WITCH PRESENTS:
TROPICAL SPELLS HOODOOS & VOODOOS

down the candle in a spiral. Set up your candle, and set any personal items of the target, or else a name paper, underneath it.

Every day for 30 minutes light the candle and command that your target be stressed, have nightmares or be unable to sleep, for thinking of you. Save the pins as they fall. Burn the candle till there's nothing left.

Next, take the pins and place them into the bottle. Also put into the bottle a personal concern, cinnamon, red ants, I Can You Can't powder, and No One But Me powder. Lid the bottle, and shake it daily or whenever you need to "remind" your target to think of you.

To Be Rid of an Old, Burdensome Relationship

You will need: Clearance Incense, Uncrossing Oil, Jinx Killer Oil, New Life Oil, Rue Soap, salt, one white candle.

Butt the candle, and carve the name of the person you want to forget on it over and over -- as many times as it will fit. Dress the candle with Uncrossing and Jinx Killer oils, and then roll it in salt. Set this up in preparation for lighting.

Light the Clearance incense and thoroughly smoke yourself in its fumes. Announce you want all ties severed, all thoughts gone, etc. Make sure to fumigate every part of your body in the incense smoke.

Once this is done, light the candle. Next, head off to the bath or shower, and thoroughly scrub yourself down with rue soap to rinse away any spiritual residue.

Finally, anoint yourself with the New Life oil on the mould of the head, on the pulse points, and on the palms of the hands and soles of the feet. Declare again, as you do so, your wish that the person be gone from you forever.

GYPSY WITCH PRESENTS: TROPICAL SPELLS HOODOOS & VOODOOS

Gambling Mojo Hand

This is reputed to be "The Best Gambling Hand" in the work attributed to Marie Laveau.

It is made by taking a 3.5 x 3.5 inch piece of chamois and fashioning it into a bag. Inside, you must place a small lodestone, a black cat bone, a swallow's heart, a pinch of five finger grass, a small John the Conqueror root, and some devil's shoestring root.

On top of all this you must place a prepared nutmeg, which is made by hollowing out a large whole nutmeg and filling it with Lady Luck Oil, then sealing it in place with wax.

With the bag filled, sew it all shut. To activate the mojo hand, apply 3 drops of Jockey Club perfume, and dress it with another 3 drops every week thereafter.

Hoodoo Candle Uncrossing Spell

If you think that an evil spell has been cast against you, dress a white offertory or pillar candle with some uncrossing oil and sprinkle with uncrossing powder. Fix the candle to the bottom of a metal pot or dish. Fill the pot or dish halfway with spring water and a cup of Holy or consecrated water. Add some dried herbs in the pot, such as agrimony, rue or basil, or maybe few cloves of garlic.

Light the candle and read the 10th Psalm and then the 37th three times. Let the candle burn itself down to the water. Pour the remains at a crossroads speaking an affirmation or chant about how you are free from evil.

GYPSY WITCH PRESENTS: TROPICAL SPELLS HOODOOS & VOODOOS

Send an Evil Spell Back to Sender

It is best to use either black or double action black candle for this spell...skull candles also work with this spell, especially if your thoughts are hexed or you have a headache.

Dress the candle with Flying Devil Oil, and sprinkle with blackberry leaf or wood betony. For a better effect, place the candle on a mirror, carve the words: "return to sender," "reverse," or something similar. Next circle the candle with crab shell powder. This will send the spell that has been cast against you back to the one who sent it as soon as the candle burns down.

Wrap the remains in old newspaper and cast into a running stream or bury in the ground away from your property

Bath for Uncrossing

Fill your bath with warm water and add the following items: Hyssop, Basil, Rue, or both, Salt, Powdered milk, a few drops of Anise oil, and a tablespoon of eggshell powder.

Read Psalms 10, 37, and 51. Immerse yourself entirely into the water or pour over your head seven or nine times. Afterwards, as the water drains away, it will take with it the evil spell that has been cast against you.

Healing and Unhexing Brew

Brew a tablespoon of nettle, a teaspoon of thyme, and a pinch of either tormentil or agrimony. Brew the herbs in spring water until boiling, then remove and cover right away. Strain and add some Holy water. Recite psalm 37 over the mixture and drink right away.

This is most effective when drunk as soon as possible after ingesting food.

GYPSY WITCH PRESENTS:
TROPICAL SPELLS HOODOOS & VOODOOS

For another good brew to heal the body and soul, take one part rosemary, one part sage, one part thyme, one part cinnamon. Half fill a blue glass bottle with clean, fresh rainwater and add the herbs and let it sit in the sun all day. Afterwards, strain the mixture and anoint the body, or add to your bath water while visualizing yourself as being in perfect health.

Psalm Prayer For Money

A simple spell to draw money and prosperity to you is to first anoint yourself with a little money drawing oil such as cedarwood or bayberry. Next, upon arising from bed, recite the 23rd psalm for seven days.

PSALM 23

The Lord is my shepherd; I shall not want.
He maketh me to lie down in green pastures.
He leadeth me beside the still waters.
He restoreth my soul.
He leadeth me in the paths of righteousness for His name's sake.
Yea, though I walk through the valley of the shadow of death,
I will fear no evil for thou art with me.
Thy rod and Thy staff they comfort me.
Thou preparest a table before me in the presence of mine enemies.
Thou anointest my head with oil.
My cup runneth over.
Surely goodness and mercy shall follow me all the days of my life, and I will dwell in the house of the Lord for ever.
Amen.

Money will arrive shortly thereafter to those who are truly deserving.

GYPSY WITCH PRESENTS:
TROPICAL SPELLS HOODOOS & VOODOOS

Divine Word to Bring Money

This is a very powerful money spell and does not require any rituals or ceremonies. Whenever you have any type of money problems and nothing is working for you, just pray these words:

YAA ALLAHO

You may say these magic words when ever you have time, while traveling, when ever you are alone.

If you are in the house and getting bored or when you are trying to sleep whenever possible just say these magic words, these words will work for you and will solve all your money problems forever.

How to Attract Success to Your Business

All of the measures below are calculated to draw customers, and thusly success, to you and your business.

In New Orleans it is believed that Saint Peter governs business because he carries keys. Get up early in the morning and light a white candle to Saint Peter. Then mix green herbs into a bucket of water...especially parsley and thyme.

Begin mopping the floor from the front of your business toward the back, moving backwards as you go. When you reach the back of your business, burn some green incense.
Get up early and burn mixture of sulfur and sugar and money drawing incense. As the sun rises, look to the east and pray for customers to be drawn to you.

Go to the graveyard and get nine handfuls of dirt. Back home, mix it with brimstone, sulfur, red pepper, and salt. Burn the mixture and pray for success in business.

GYPSY WITCH PRESENTS:
TROPICAL SPELLS HOODOOS & VOODOOS

Divine Guardian Angel Spell

Place three candles surrounded by sugar on a plate at the highest point in your home. Light the candles and ask for three wishes to the three guardian angels Rafael, Michael and Gabriel. One wish for success, one wish for prosperity and one impossible wish. Repeat this spell for three days.

If your wishes come through, publish your thanks to your guardian angels in the classified ads in the local newspaper.

Bible Verse to Rid Yourself of Money Woes

Repeat this Bible verse once a day to free yourself from any problems with money.

I will also make it a possession for the bittern, and pools of water: and I will sweep it with the besom of destruction, saith the LORD of hosts.

Isaiah 14:23

GYPSY WITCH PRESENTS:
TROPICAL SPELLS HOODOOS & VOODOOS

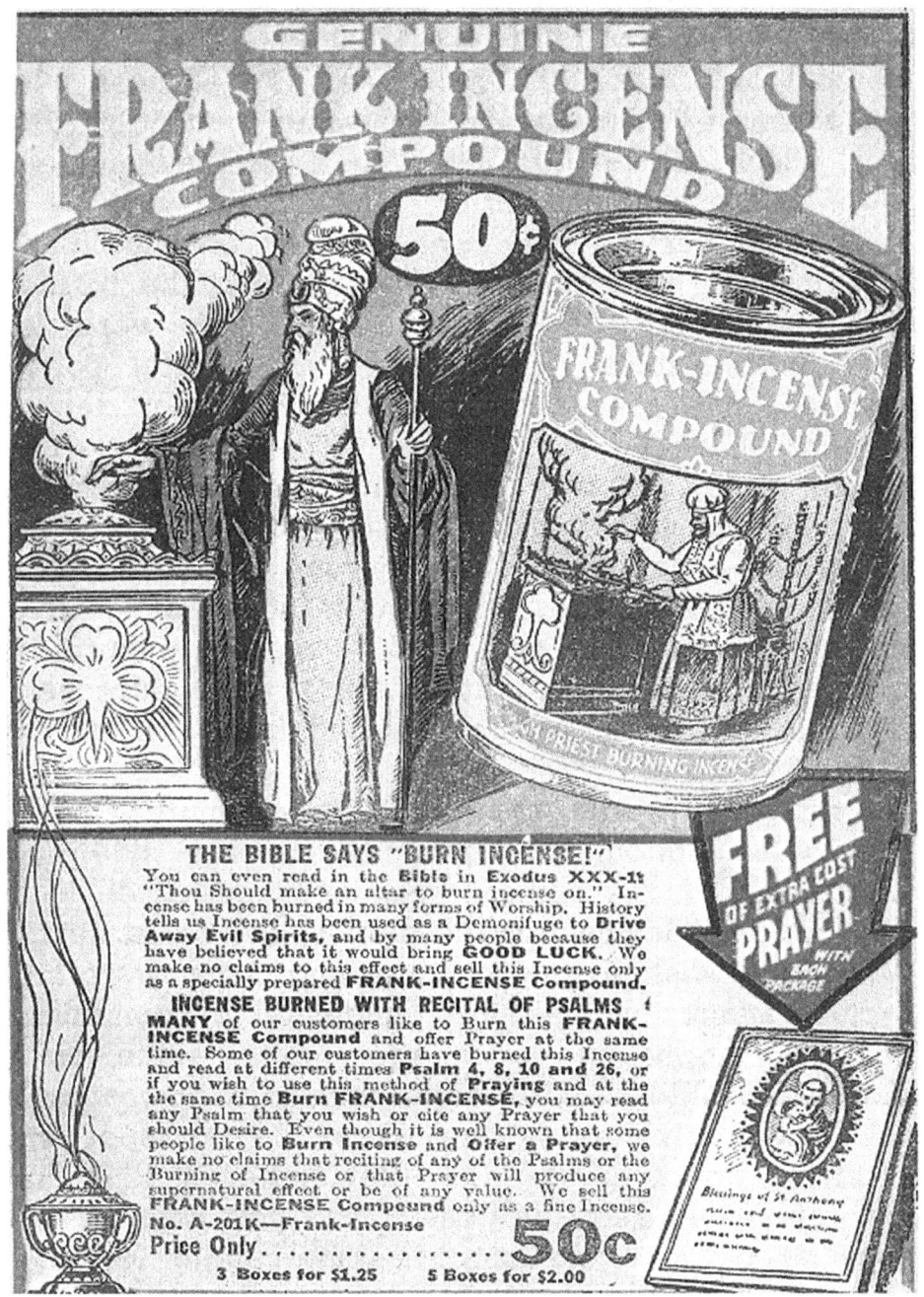

From Hoodoo Curio Catalog, King Novelty Co. 1944

GYPSY WITCH PRESENTS:
TROPICAL SPELLS HOODOOS & VOODOOS

PART FOUR
Conjure Powers With The Bible

A great soul once asked: "Why curse the darkness when you can light a candle?" The ritualistic burning of candles is a form of prayer, which can be performed in a complex and elaborate manner, or in the simplest form.

In this chapter we will explore only the simplified forms of candle magick because we are combining the magickal art of candle burning with the invocation of Divine words and the power of Bible Verses. This extremely powerful combination will serve a conjurer as a most powerful tool for dealing with the problems of life.

Before you begin, two things must be considered for your hoodoo spell: Do you wish to attract, or repel? When you want to attract a certain thing into your life such as healing, good fortune, money, love, etc., you must prepare the candle by applying oil to it as you hold a mental picture of your desire. Some use olive oil, others use special purpose oil for anointing candles which can be obtained from spiritual/new age supply stores.

To anoint a candle to attract, the conjurer must apply some oil to the bottom of the candle on one side, then rub upward and stop at the center. Then one applies oil to the top of the candle, rub downward and stop at the same center spot.

When you wish to repel something from your life, such as psychic attack, ill fortune, undesirable conditions and situations etc., apply oil as follows: Apply some oil to the center of the candle on one side, then rub downward to the bottom. Then apply oil to the same center spot and rub upward to the tip of the candle. Remember, it is best to use only one candle for each purpose. Once you prepare a candle for a special purpose, do not use that candle for any other reason.

When the candle has burned down to a stub, you should dispose of it properly. Some wrap the leftover wax in a piece of cloth and bury it. Others prefer to throw it into running water. Others throw the entire wax into a larger fire so that all is consumed. You may select the method that suits you.

Depending on what it is that you hope to achieve with

GYPSY WITCH PRESENTS:
TROPICAL SPELLS HOODOOS & VOODOOS

your spell, choose an appropriately colored candle. Remember, if you only have one color of candle, a white candle can be used for any type of spell.

Decide if your spell is supposed to attract or repel. You then need to anoint the candle and carve upon it the Divine Name of Power based on attraction or repelling. To carve the Divine Names of Power on candles is a form of silent invocation to the power within that name.

Since the fall of man, Angelic Beings have communicated to the human race certain formulas by which humanity could regain the lost power of its original state. One such communication is Divine Names of Power meant to illuminate the mystical process. The Divine Names of Power are hidden within the Scriptures, and when written or spoken in a certain way, release an awesome power for great accomplishments.

One Divine Name of Power will attract, the other name is to repel. The Divine Name for attraction is: **SCHADDEI**.

The Divine Name for repelling is: **AHA HE**.

I recommend that you use something made of clean metal to carve the Divine Name of Power. An unused pin or needle works well. If your candle is large enough, a sharp knife can be used. It is best not to repeat the Divine Names of Power out loud, unless you are able to pronounce them in the Hebrew language correctly.

After you have prepared your candle and carved the Divine Name of Power, the practitioner must then light the candle and begin the ritual. As always, choose to do your Bible Verse spell in a quiet location free of any distractions.

The first step of the ritual is to repeat the prescribed Bible verse out loud. What follows should be a sincere prayer, asking for the desired help in accomplishing your special purpose. Be sure to pray in your own words, for then the prayer will come from the heart.

Finally, one should remain in silent meditation on desired results for a few moments before closing the ritual. As you select the various Bible Verses to improve your condition, you must do so with a feeling of expectancy and an attitude of faith that you will receive the desired help from the universal Creative Force.

When you complete your session, do not think too much

GYPSY WITCH PRESENTS:
TROPICAL SPELLS HOODOOS & VOODOOS

about it or worry as to how your help will come. Just be at ease, trying to be aware of opportunities that may arise in your daily life. Repeat a ritual for a specific purpose as often as possible, until you see the desired results. Keep a positive attitude and speak in a more positive manner.

Allow the candle to burn completely out and dispose of it properly. This will signify the end of your spell.

Here is a chart of basic candle color symbolism as they relate to Hoodoo:

Red - affection, passion, energy/vigor, sexuality, often used in love spells

Orange - changing plans, prophetic dreams, making a way/opening the doors of opportunity

Yellow - prayer, devotion, attraction, joyfulness, money (used to substitute for gold)

Green - gambling, business, jobs, crops, money spells

Blue - joy, harmony, peace, good intentions, healing/health

Purple - control, command, domination, power, mastery

Black – sorrow, freedom from evil/oppression, absorption of negativity, cursing/jinxing/hexing, removal of curse/jinx/hex

White – spirituality, blessings, healing, rest, rejuvenation, refreshing

Brown - neutral, "earthy energy," court case spells (often)

Pink - attraction, romance (often used in love spells)

GYPSY WITCH PRESENTS: TROPICAL SPELLS HOODOOS & VOODOOS

TO HAVE GOOD LUCK

Prepare a green candle to attract.

He is the image of the invisible God, the firstborn of all creation. For by him all things were created, in heaven and on earth, visible and invisible, whether thrones or dominions or rulers or authorities—all things were created through him and for him.

Colossians 1:15-16

NEW LOVE AND ROMANCE

Prepare a pink candle to attract.

*Fear not, for I am with you;
be not dismayed, for I am your God;
I will strengthen you, I will help you,
I will uphold you with my righteous right hand.*

Isaiah 41:10

GOOD FORTUNE IN BUSINESS AND MONEY

Prepare a green candle to attract.

*God is not man, that he should lie,
or a son of man, that he should change his mind.
Has he said, and will he not do it?
Or has he spoken, and will he not fulfill it?*

Numbers 23:19

GYPSY WITCH PRESENTS:
TROPICAL SPELLS HOODOOS & VOODOOS

KEEP SOMEONE AWAY

Prepare a purple candle to repel.

For am I now seeking the approval of man, or of God? Or am I trying to please man? If I were still trying to please man, I would not be a servant of Christ.

Galatians 1:10

TO ATTRACT GOOD HEALTH

Prepare a blue candle to attract.

I said to the boastful, 'Do not deal boastfully,' And to the wicked, 'Do not lift up the horn, Do not lift up your horn on high; Do not speak with a stiff neck,' For exaltation comes neither from the east Nor from the west nor from the south, But God is the Judge: He puts down one, And exalts another.

Psalm 75:4-7

TO SEND AWAY BAD HEALTH

Prepare a white candle to repel.

Do not think that I came to destroy the Law or the Prophets; I did not come to destroy but to fulfill; For assuredly, I say to you, till heaven and earth pass away, one jot or one tittle will by no means pass from the law till all is fulfilled.

Matthew 5:17-18

PROTECTION WHILE TRAVELING

Prepare a purple candle to repel.

GYPSY WITCH PRESENTS:
TROPICAL SPELLS HOODOOS & VOODOOS

He drew a circular horizon on the face of the waters, At the boundary of light and darkness, The pillars of heaven tremble.

Job 26:10-14

TO RID YOURSELF OF A BOTHERSOME LOVER

Prepare a pink candle to repel.

May the glory of the Lord endure forever; May the Lord rejoice in His works, He looks on the earth, and it trembles; He touches the hills, and they smoke" I will sing to the Lord as long as I live; I will sing praise to my God while I have my being.

Psalms 104:31-33

TO GAIN TRUST AND FAVOR

Prepare a white candle to attract.

For the word of God is living and powerful, and sharper than any two-edged sword, piercing even to the division of soul and spirit, and of joints and marrow, and is a discerner of the thoughts and intents of the heart; And there is no creature hidden from His sight, but all things are naked and open to the eyes of Him to whom we must give account.

Hebrews 4:12-13

REMOVE A CURSE

Prepare a purple candle to repel.

Now to the King eternal, immortal, invisible, to God who alone

GYPSY WITCH PRESENTS:
TROPICAL SPELLS HOODOOS & VOODOOS

is wise, be honor and glory forever and ever, Amen.

1 Timothy 1:17

MAKE GOOD WISHES COME TRUE

Prepare a red candle to attract.

Many, O LORD my God, are Your wonderful works Which You have done; And Your thoughts toward us Cannot be recounted to You in order; If I would declare and speak of them, They are more than can be numbered.

Psalms 40:5

BRING BACK A LOST LOVER

Prepare a pink candle to attract.

Ask, and it will be given to you; seek, and you will find; knock, and it will be opened to you. For everyone who asks receives, and the one who seeks finds, and to the one who knocks it will be opened.

Matthew 7:7-8

TO REMOVE THE EVIL EYE

Prepare a white candle to repel.

And it is God who establishes us with you in Christ, and has anointed us, and who has also put his seal on us and given us his Spirit in our hearts as a guarantee.

2 Corinthians 1:21-22

GYPSY WITCH PRESENTS:
TROPICAL SPELLS HOODOOS & VOODOOS

HELP A FRIEND WHO IS DEPRESSED

Prepare a blue candle to attract.

Do not love the world or the things in the world. If anyone loves the world, the love of the Father is not in him. For all that is in the world—the desires of the flesh and the desires of the eyes and pride in possessions—is not from the Father but is from the world. And the world is passing away along with its desires, but whoever does the will of God abides forever.

1 John 2:15-17

TO GAIN SPIRITUAL POWER

Prepare a purple candle to attract.

And they did bind the breastplate by his rings unto the rings of the ephod with a lace of blue, that it might be above the curious girdle of the ephod, and that the breastplate might not be loosed from the ephod; as the Lord commanded Moses.

Exodus 39:21

TO OVERCOME A STRONG ENEMY

Prepare a purple candle to repel.

And now thou sayest, Go, tell thy lord, Behold, Elijah is here.

1 Kings 18:11

TO MAKE GOOD FRIENDS

Prepare a red candle to attract.

GYPSY WITCH PRESENTS:
TROPICAL SPELLS HOODOOS & VOODOOS

Again, think ye that we excuse ourselves unto you? We speak before God in Christ: but we do all things, dearly beloved, for your edifying.

2 Corinthians 12:19

END AN ARGUMENT

Prepare a purple candle to repel.

And set up false witnesses, which said, This man ceaseth not to speak blasphemous words against this holy place, and the law.

Acts 6:13

GAIN FORGIVENESS

Prepare a blue candle to attract.

And he said unto them, I am an Hebrew; and I fear the Lord, the God of heaven, which hath made the sea and the dry land.

Jonah 1:9

FOR RECONCILIATION

Prepare a blue candle to attract.

And I will set the Egyptians against the Egyptians: and they shall fight every one against his brother, and every one against his neighbor; city against city, and kingdom against kingdom.

Isaiah 19:2

GYPSY WITCH PRESENTS:
TROPICAL SPELLS HOODOOS & VOODOOS

MAKE SOMEONE DREAM OF YOU

Prepare a white candle to attract.

My soul hath kept thy testimonies; and I love them exceedingly.

Psalms 119:167

TO TURN AN ENEMY INTO A FRIEND

Prepare a purple candle to attract.

A time to cast away stones, and a time to gather stones together; a time to embrace, and a time to refrain from embracing.

Ecclesiastes 3:5

CLEANSE A HOME FROM NEGATIVE ENERGY

Prepare a white candle to repel.

That it might be fulfilled which was spoken by the prophet, saying, I will open my mouth in parables; I will utter things which have been kept secret from the foundation of the world.

Matthew 13:35

RID HOME OF TROUBLESOME SPIRITS

Prepare white candle to repel.

And that which thou sowest, thou sowest not that body that shall be, but bare grain, it may chance of wheat, or of some other grain.
1 Corinthians 15:37

GYPSY WITCH PRESENTS:
TROPICAL SPELLS HOODOOS & VOODOOS

ENHANCE YOUR POWERS PHYSICALLY AND MENTALLY

Prepare a red candle to attract.

And I will encamp about mine house because of the army, because of him that passeth by, and because of him that returneth: and no oppressor shall pass through them any more: for now have I seen with mine eyes.

Zechariah 9:8

TO GAIN INNER STRENGTH

Prepare a blue candle to attract.

But grow in grace, and in the knowledge of our Lord and Saviour Jesus Christ. To him be glory both now and for ever. Amen.

2 Peter 3:18

FOR WISDOM AND KNOWLEDGE

Prepare a green candle to attract.

Every valley shall be filled, and every mountain and hill shall be brought low; and the crooked shall be made straight, and the rough ways shall be made smooth.

Luke 3:5

TO LOSE YOUR TROUBLES

Prepare a blue candle to repel.

And Pharaoh said unto him, Get thee from me, take heed to

GYPSY WITCH PRESENTS:
TROPICAL SPELLS HOODOOS & VOODOOS

thyself, see my face no more; for in that day thou seest my face thou shalt die.

Exodus 10:28

REMOVE BAD LUCK AND ALL CURSES

Prepare a white candle to repel.

Nevertheless they were disobedient, and rebelled against thee, and cast thy law behind their backs, and slew thy prophets which testified against them to turn them to thee, and they wrought great provocations.

Nehemiah 9:26

TO RECEIVE AN ANSWER TO A QUESTION

Prepare a blue candle to attract.

Woe is me! for I am as when they have gathered the summer fruits, as the grapegleanings of the vintage: there is no cluster to eat: my soul desired the firstripe fruit.

Micah 7:1

TO GET A BETTER JOB

Prepare a green candle to attract.

For the Lamb which is in the midst of the throne shall feed them, and shall lead them unto living fountains of waters: and God shall wipe away all tears from their eyes.

Revelation 7:17

GYPSY WITCH PRESENTS: TROPICAL SPELLS HOODOOS & VOODOOS

FOR SUCCESS IN BUSINESS

Prepare a green candle to attract.

They shall be abundantly satisfied with the fatness of thy house; and thou shalt make them drink of the river of thy pleasures.

Psalms 36:8

RID YOURSELF OF TROUBLES WITH MONEY OR BUSINESS

Prepare a green candle to repel.

I will also make it a possession for the bittern, and pools of water: and I will sweep it with the besom of destruction, saith the LORD of hosts.

Isaiah 14:23

STOP YOUR BOSS FROM BOTHERING YOU

Prepare a purple candle to repel.

Yet will I leave a remnant, that ye may have some that shall escape the sword among the nations, when ye shall be scattered through the countries.

Ezekiel 6:8

TO GET BETTER WORK FROM EMPLOYEES

Prepare a purple candle to attract.

Lord, my heart is not haughty, nor mine eyes lofty: neither do I exercise myself in great matters, or in things too high for me. – Psalms 131:1

GYPSY WITCH PRESENTS: TROPICAL SPELLS HOODOOS & VOODOOS

RISE ABOVE ANY COMPETITION

Prepare a red candle to attract.

A wise king scattereth the wicked, and bringeth the wheel over them.

Proverbs 20:26

SUCCESS FROM UNFAIR COMPETITION

Prepare a red candle to repel.

The wrath of God came upon them, and slew the fattest of them, and smote down the chosen men of Israel.

Psalms 78:31

TO ATTRACT CUSTOMERS

Prepare a green candle to attract.

And the multitudes gave heed with one accord unto the things that were spoken by Philip, when they heard, and saw the signs which he did.

Acts 8:6

TO RID YOURSELF OF BAD DREAMS

Prepare a white candle to repel.

and those that weep, as though they wept not; and those that rejoice, as though they rejoiced not; and those that buy, as though they possessed not;

1 Corinthians 7:30

GYPSY WITCH PRESENTS:
TROPICAL SPELLS HOODOOS & VOODOOS

TO RID SOMEONE ELSE OF BAD DREAMS

Prepare a white candle to repel.

My heart fluttereth, horror hath affrighted me; the twilight that I desired hath been turned into trembling unto me.

Isaiah 21:4

TO HAVE A NIGHT OF PLEASANT DREAMS

Prepare a white candle to attract.

And I will lay thy flesh upon the mountains, and fill the valleys with thy height.

Ezekiel 32:5

TO HAVE A TROUBLE FREE NIGHT OF SLEEP

Prepare a white candle to attract.

And when the dew that lay was gone up, behold, upon the face of the wilderness a small round thing, small as the hoarfrost on the ground.
Exodus 16:14

ALWAYS AWAKEN FRESH AND FULL OF ENERGY

Prepare a red candle to attract.

And so it was, when the cloud abode from even unto the morning, and that the cloud was taken up in the morning, then they journeyed: whether it was by day or by night that the cloud was taken up, they journeyed.

Numbers 9:21

GYPSY WITCH PRESENTS:
TROPICAL SPELLS HOODOOS & VOODOOS

STOP A LOVER FROM CHEATING

Prepare a pink candle to attract.

through whom also we have had our access by faith into this grace wherein we stand; and we rejoice in hope of the glory of God.

Romans 5:2

STOP SOMEONE FROM STEALING YOUR LOVER

Prepare a pink candle to repel.

When I say unto the wicked, Thou shalt surely die; and thou givest him not warning, nor speakest to warn the wicked from his wicked way, to save his life; the same wicked man shall die in his iniquity; but his blood will I require at thy hand.

Ezekiel 3:18

REKINDLE THE FIRE IN A ROMANCE

Prepare a red candle to attract.

For to do whatsoever thy hand and thy counsel determined before to be done.

Acts 4:28

TO BE A BETTER LOVER

Prepare a red candle to attract.

And call upon me in the day of trouble; I will deliver thee, and thou shalt glorify me.
Psalms 50:15

GYPSY WITCH PRESENTS: TROPICAL SPELLS HOODOOS & VOODOOS

TO HAVE YOUR PARTNER BE A BETTER LOVER

Prepare a red candle to attract.

He brought me forth also into a large place; He delivered me, because he delighted in me.

Psalms 18:19

FIND A BETTER LOVER

Prepare a red candle to attract.

For this is he, of whom it is written, Behold, I send my messenger before thy face, which shall prepare thy way before thee.

Matthew 11:10

CONTACT YOUR GUARDIAN ANGEL

Prepare a purple candle to attract.

They are of the world: therefore speak they of the world, and the world heareth them.

1 John 4:5

CONTACT AN ASCENDED MASTER

Prepare a white candle to attract.

For he shall never be moved; The righteous shall be had in everlasting remembrance.

Psalms 112:6

GYPSY WITCH PRESENTS: TROPICAL SPELLS HOODOOS & VOODOOS

CONTACT YOUR SPIRIT GUIDE

Prepare a purple candle to attract.

Whom I have sent unto you for the same purpose, that ye might know our affairs, and that he might comfort your hearts.

Ephesians 6:22

PROTECTION FROM MALEVOLENT SPIRITS

Prepare a purple candle to repel.

From above hath he sent fire into my bones, and it prevaileth against them: he hath spread a net for my feet, he hath turned me back: he hath made me desolate and faint all the day.

Lamentations 1:13

TO HELP A TROUBLED SOUL FIND PEACE

Prepare a pink candle to attract.

From above hath he sent fire into my bones, and it prevaileth against them: he hath spread a net for my feet, he hath turned me back: he hath made me desolate and faint all the day.

Lamentations 1:13

TO GAIN PROSPECTIVE IN THE FACE OF DIFFICULTY

Prepare a blue candle to attract.

Now therefore, our God, the great, the mighty, and the terrible God, who keepest covenant and lovingkindness, let not all the travail seem little before thee, that hath come upon us, on our kings, on our princes, and on our priests, and on our prophets,

GYPSY WITCH PRESENTS: TROPICAL SPELLS HOODOOS & VOODOOS

and on our fathers, and on all thy people, since the time of the kings of Assyria unto this day.

Nehemiah 9:32

TO BRING JOY AND HAPPINESS TO YOUR FAMILY

Prepare a green candle to attract.

I communed with mine own heart, saying, Lo, I have gotten me great wisdom above all that were before me in Jerusalem; yea, my heart hath had great experience of wisdom and knowledge.

Ecclesiastes 1:16

Hoodoo Prayer to Heal Anyone from Attacks by Evil Spirits

Thou unclean spirit, thou has attacked (Name); let that evil recede from him into thy marrow and into thy bone, let it be returned unto thee. I exorcise thee for the sake of the five wounds of Jesus, thou evil spirit, and conjure thee for the five wounds of Jesus of this flesh, marrow and bone; I exorcise thee for the sake of the five wounds of Jesus, at this very hour restore to health again (Name), in the name of God the Father, God the Son, and of God the Holy Spirit.

Hoodoo Prayer to Forever Banish Wicked People

All ye evil spirits, I forbid you my bedstead, my couch; I forbid you, in the name of God, my house and home; I forbid you, in the name of the Holy Trinity, my blood and flesh, my body and soul; I forbid you all the nail holes in my house and home, till you have traveled over every hillock, waded through every water, have counted all the leaflets of the trees, and counted all the starlets in the sky, until that beloved day arrives when the mother of God will bring forth her second Son.

GYPSY WITCH PRESENTS:
TROPICAL SPELLS HOODOOS & VOODOOS

This formula, three times spoken in the house of the person whom we seek to aid is always very effective.

Hoodoo Prayer against Trouble in General

Repeat reverently, and with sincere faith, the following words, and you shall be protected in the hour of danger:

He shall deliver thee in six troubles, yea, in seven there shall no evil touch thee; in famine he shall redeem thee from death, and in war from the power of the sword; and thou shall know that thy tabernacle shall be in peace, and thou shalt visit thy habitation and shall not err.

GYPSY WITCH PRESENTS:
TROPICAL SPELLS HOODOOS & VOODOOS

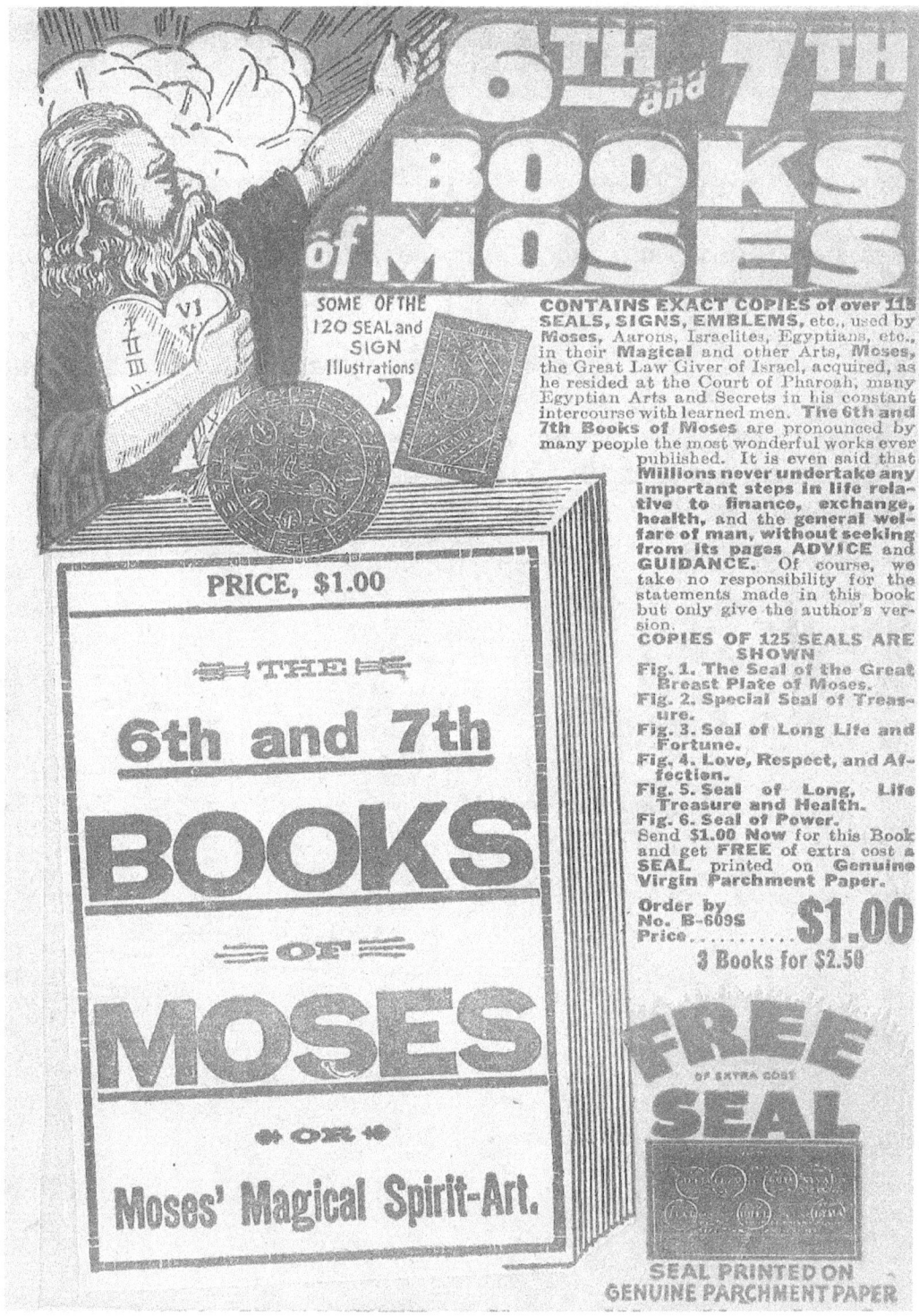

From Hoodoo Curio Catalog, King Novelty Co. 1944

GYPSY WITCH PRESENTS:
TROPICAL SPELLS HOODOOS & VOODOOS

PART FIVE
Hoodoo With The Psalms

Hoodoo conjuring has a strong Old Testament tradition. This is particularly evident in relation to God's providence and his role in retributive justice. For example, though there are strong ideas of good versus evil, cursing someone to cause their death might not be considered a malignant act. Not only is God's providence a factor in hoodoo practice, but hoodoo thought understands God, himself, as the archetypal hoodoo doctor.

With hoodoo, it is considered that the Bible is the first and greatest conjure book in the world. It has many functions for the hoodoo conjurer, especially as a source for spells. This is particularly true with the Psalms in which it is believed that they contain "seed sounds" or hidden syllables which, when spoken aloud, will cause magickal works to be accomplished. The magickal effect produced by the scripture is directly related to the subject-matter of the passage.

Among the many results that proper recitation of the specific Psalms will produce are release from prison, safe childbirth, business success, safe travel, help in court cases, removal of enemies, and overcoming evil.

There have been a number of different interpretations on the mystical meanings of the Psalms over the years, but, in hoodoo tradition, all seem to stay within a similar framework. Here is a list of the magickal keys of the Psalms as compiled by William Oribello.

Psalm 1   For a normal timely delivery.
Psalm 2   When confronted with a storm of the sea.
Psalm 3   For a severe headache or backache.
Psalm 4   To bring good luck.
Psalm 5   To gain favor with persons of authority.
Psalm 6   To heal the eyes.
Psalm 7   To overcome evil caused by your enemies.
Psalm 8   To win favor in business transactions.
Psalm 9   For a sick child.
Psalm 10 To remove evil or restless spirits.

GYPSY WITCH PRESENTS: TROPICAL SPELLS HOODOOS & VOODOOS

Psalm 11   To overcome fear and slander.
Psalm 12   To rise above gossip from enemies.
Psalm 13   To remain safe for twenty four hours.
Psalm 14   To gain trust and favor.
Psalm 15   To overcome depression.
Psalm 16   To be happy.
Psalm 17   For a safe journey.
Psalm 18   To overcome attackers and robbers.
Psalm 19   To overcome a serious, confining illness.
Psalm 20   To overcome danger and suffering for a day.
Psalm 21   To repel a storm at sea.
Psalm 22   To repel bad luck.
Psalm 23   To receive instructions in dreams.
Psalms 24 & 25 To receive great strength in the face of opposition.
Psalm 26   Against dangers from nature on land or sea.
Psalm 27   To be accepted in a strange or new place.
Psalm 28   To gain peace with a person you have had a falling out with.
Psalm 29   To overpower an evil spirit.
Psalm 30   For power and safety.
Psalm 31   Against slander.
Psalm 32   For Divine Grace, Love and Mercy.
Psalm 33   To prevent the death of young children.
Psalm 34   To obtain favors from important people.
Psalms 35 & 36 To gain favor in court cases.
Psalm 37   To overcome alcoholism.
Psalms 38 & 39 To overcome slander.
Psalm 40   To free oneself from evil oppression.
Psalms 41, 42 & 43 To regain credibility after being slandered.
Psalm 44   To be safe from enemies.
Psalms 45 & 46 To restore peace and love in relationships.
Psalm 47   To be loved.
Psalm 48   To overcome those who envy you.
Psalms 49 & 50 To overcome fever.
Psalm 51   To be free of guilt.
Psalm 52   To rise above slander.
Psalms 53, 54, & 55 To overcome persecution by enemies.
Psalm 56   To overcome materiality.

GYPSY WITCH PRESENTS:
TROPICAL SPELLS HOODOOS & VOODOOS

Psalm 57   To attract good fortune.
Psalm 58   For peaceable communion with animals and nature.
Psalm 59   Against possession of an evil spirit.
Psalm 60   To remain safe during war.
Psalm 61   To have many blessings when moving into a new home.
Psalm 62   To find forgiveness in your heart.
Psalm 63   To be free of a business deal.
Psalm 64   To have a safe and successful Journey.
Psalm 65   To have good luck when seeking a better job.
Psalm 66   Against negative obsessions and compulsions.
Psalms 67 & 68 To not be brought down by bad events.
Psalms 69 & 70 To break unclean habits.
Psalm 71   To help release one from bondage.
Psalm 72   To have happiness in all types of relationships.
Psalms 73 to 83 These eleven Psalms are all purpose Psalms.
Psalm 84   To overcome chronic illness and bad odors.
Psalm 85   To restore peace between you and someone.
Psalms 86, 87 & 88   To bring success to others.
Psalm 89   for absentee healing.
Psalm 90   For protection in your dwelling.
Psalm 91 Against incurable disease or evil spirits.
Psalm 92   To help yourself be honorable.
Psalm 93   For aid in court cases.
Psalm 94   To gain power over an enemy.
Psalm 95   To help friends who are about to make a grave error.
Psalms 96 & 97 To bring happiness and blessings to your family.
Psalm 98   To establish peace among the members of your family.
Psalm 99   To develop inner power.
Psalm 100 To conquer unknown enemies.
Psalm 101 Against the Evil Eye.
Psalms 102 & 103 For fertility.
Psalm 104 To break free from melancholy.
Psalms 105, 106, & 107 To get rid of fevers.
Psalm 108   To have a bountiful home life.
Psalm 109 To overcome a strong enemy.
Psalms 110 & 111 To have charm.

GYPSY WITCH PRESENTS:
TROPICAL SPELLS HOODOOS & VOODOOS

Psalms 112 & 113 To develop self balance and harmony.
Psalm 114 For a successful business venture.
Psalm 115 To teach.
Psalm 116 For safety.
Psalm 117 To help you keep your word.
Psalm 118 To have positive willpower.
Psalm 119 - Verses 1 thru 8   To help cure shaking limbs.
Psalm 119 Verses 9 thru 16 To gain intelligence and improve memory.
Psalm 119 - Verses 17 thru 24   To help cure eye problems of another.
Psalm 119 - Verses 25 thru 32   To help cure the left eye.
Psalm 119 - Verses 33 thru 40   To aid one's spiritual life.
Psalm 119 Verses 41 thru 48   To be a positive influence for another.
Psalm 119 - Verses 49 thru 56   To help a friend conquer melancholy.
Psalm 119 - Verses 57 thru 64   To cure pains in the upper part of the body.
Psalm 119 - Verses 65 thru 72   To cure hip pains, kidney or liver problems.
Psalm 119 - Verses 73 thru 80   To obtain favor with humans.
Psalm 119 - Verses 81 thru 88   To help cure a burning sore or swelling of the nose.
Psalm 119 - Verses 89 thru 96 To achieve justice in court cases.
Psalm 119 - Verses 97 thru 104 To relieve pain in the limbs or hands.
Psalm 119 - Verses 105 thru 112 To have a safe journey.
Psalm 119 - Verses 113 thru 120   To help one talking with a superior.
Psalm 119 - Verses 121 thru 128 To cure pain in the left arm and hands.
Psalm 119 - verses 137 thru 144 To receive intuitive guidance.
Psalm 119 - Verses 145 thru 152   To cure pain in the leg.
Psalm 119 - Verses 153 thru 160   To cure a boil in the ear.
Psalm 119 Verses 161 thru 168 To cure headaches.
Psalm 120 To receive justice in court.
Psalm 121 For safety during travel at night
Psalm 122 For favor when approaching a person of authority.

GYPSY WITCH PRESENTS:
TROPICAL SPELLS HOODOOS & VOODOOS

Psalm 124 For a safe journey by water.
Psalm 125 To gain power when enemies seem to overpower you.
Psalm 126 & 127 To bless and protect children.
Psalm 128 To protect a pregnancy.
Psalm 129 To achieve spiritual power.
Psalm 131 To overcome pride.
Psalm 132 To gain the ability to keep your word.
Psalm 133 To gain and keep true friends.
Psalm 136 To break cycles of negativity.
Psalm 137 To overcome resentment.
Psalm 138 To attract love and friendship.
Psalm 139 To deepen the love between couples.
Psalm 140 To eliminate marriage problems.
Psalm 141 To get rid of fear.
Psalms 142 & 143 To relieve pain in the arms and legs.
Psalm 144 To speed the healing of broken limbs.
Psalm 145 To banish evil spirits.
Psalm 146 To cure a wound.
Psalm 147 To cure infections.
Psalms 148 & 149 To prevent destructive fire.
Psalm 150 To turn sadness into glee.

Psalm for Obtaining Work

Use one teaspoon full of olive oil into a very clean jar of holy water say the 26th Psalm over it. Anoint yourself with this oil when applying for a job or looking for work.

Psalm 26

Vindicate me, O LORD, for I have led a blameless life; I have trusted in the LORD without wavering. Test me, O LORD, and try me, examine my heart and my mind; for your love is ever before me, and I walk continually in your truth.

I do not sit with deceitful men, nor do I consort with hypocrites; I abhor the assembly of evildoers and refuse to sit with the wicked.

GYPSY WITCH PRESENTS:
TROPICAL SPELLS HOODOOS & VOODOOS

I wash my hands in innocence, and go about your altar, O LORD, proclaiming aloud your praise and telling of all your wonderful deeds.

I love the house where you live, O LORD, the place where your glory dwells.

Do not take away my soul along with sinners, my life with bloodthirsty men, in whose hands are wicked schemes, whose right hands are full of bribes.

But I lead a blameless life; redeem me and be merciful to me.

My feet stand on level ground; in the great assembly I will praise the LORD.

Psalm 91- So That Nothing May Harm You

Read the 91 Psalm twice a day at 12 o clock. Read it at noon, and when you go to bed. Afterwards, ask God to take care of you so that nothing will ever harm you.

Psalm 91

He that dwelleth in the secret place of the Most High shall abide under the shadow of the Almighty.

I will say of the LORD, He is my refuge and my fortress: my God; in him will I trust.

Surely he shall deliver thee from the snare of the fowler, and from the noisome pestilence.

He shall cover thee with his feathers, and under his wings shalt thou trust: his truth shall be thy shield and buckler.

Thou shalt not be afraid for the terror by night; nor for the arrow that flieth by day; nor for the pestilence that walketh in darkness; nor for the destruction that wasteth at noonday.

GYPSY WITCH PRESENTS: TROPICAL SPELLS HOODOOS & VOODOOS

A thousand shall fall at thy side, and ten thousand at thy right hand; but it shall not come nigh thee.

Only with thine eyes shalt thou behold and see the reward of the wicked.

Because thou hast made the LORD, which is my refuge, even the Most High, thy habitation; there shall no evil befall thee, neither shall any plague come nigh thy dwelling.

For he shall give his angels charge over thee, to keep thee in all thy ways.
They shall bear thee up in their hands, lest thou dash thy foot against a stone.

Thou shalt tread upon the lion and adder: the young lion and the dragon shalt thou trample under feet.

Because he hath set his love upon me, therefore will I deliver him: I will set him on high, because he hath known my name.

He shall call upon me, and I will answer him: I will be with him in trouble; I will deliver him, and honor him.

With long life will I satisfy him, and show him my salvation.

Fiery Wall of Protection Spell

This spell will invoke the aid of Archangel Michael and his flaming sword.

Ingredients: four blue candles, one white candle, one black candle, angelica root, Dragon's Blood incense, a handful of graveyard dirt, Hot Foot Powder, Fiery Wall of Protection Powder, Fiery Wall of Protection Oil, one Saint Michael medal, One coffin nail, Name paper, if possible, a personal item of the person that you need protection from.

Begin by cleansing the area of any negativity that might be

GYPSY WITCH PRESENTS:
TROPICAL SPELLS HOODOOS & VOODOOS

hanging around. Burn Dragon's Blood and go around the room clock-wise, smoking the area. Place a pinch of Fiery Wall of Protection Powder in the four corners of the room.

On your altar, or a safe, clean work area set your supplies. Put the graveyard dirt in a glass bowl. Carve the word protection in the white candle, using the coffin nail. Dress this candle with Fiery Wall of Protection Oil.
Place your Saint Michael medal next to this candle. As you dress the candle, say: "*Protect me with your fiery sword,*" (or the name of the person you are working the spell for). Set this candle down and sprinkle a protective circle around it three times using first: Fiery Wall of Protection Powder, second: Angelica root pieces, third: five finger grass. Light the candle.

Next, take the four blue candles and carve the name of the Archangels: *Michael, Gabriel, Raphael*, and *Uriel*. One name of each archangel on each blue candle. Dress these candles with Fiery Wall of Protection Oil as you say each of their names.

You can chant: "*Michael, Michael, burning bright, protect me now with all your might.*" Repeat this chant for each of the four archangels.

Place these four blue candles (one north, one south, one east, and one west) around the white candle. Place them on top of the circle of powder and herbs, and light all four of the blue candles.

Take your paper and write the name of the person or thing that you seek protection from three times. Sprinkle some hot foot powder (just a pinch) on the paper. Fold the name paper up to as small as you can make it, always folding away from yourself as you do it.

Take the black candle and carve "keep away" on one side. On the other side carve the persons name. Light this candle, and as it burns recite Psalm 91. Take the name paper and touch it to the flame on the black candle. Place it on top of the graveyard dirt and let it burn. When it has burned down to

GYPSY WITCH PRESENTS:
TROPICAL SPELLS HOODOOS & VOODOOS

ashes, take the black candle and set it on top of the ashes. Let it burn all the way down, or for as long as you are able to safely let it burn before extinguishing it.

Let the Blue and white candles burn down. Take the Saint Michael card or medal and some of the herbs and powder and place them in a blue cloth or mojo bag. Dress it with Fiery Wall of Protection Oil and carry it with you.

Take the candle, ashes and graveyard dirt to a cemetery and bury them there. Or else take them to a crossroads and throw everything into the middle of the crossroad over your left shoulder, walk away, and don't look back.

Afterwards, take a cleansing protection bath using hyssop and eucalyptus afterwards. As you pour the water over you recite Psalm 37.

Lover Call Me

Items you will need: matches, glass cup, water, Bible turned to Psalm 40, a washcloth with a circle cut in the middle. Spell is to be done only between the hours of 4:00AM and 5:00AM.

Pour the water in the glass. Put the cloth over the glass making sure that the middle of it is in the middle of the glass. Have your Bible turned to Psalm 40.

Say: *"(name of lover) I bid you come to me in the name of the father, the son, and the Holy Spirit."*

Light one match and repeat several times.

Next say: *"In the name of the father, (name of lover) I bid you come to me."*

Quickly drop the match into the water. Then concentrate on the lover. Light another match, now say, *"In the name of the son, (name of lover) I bid you come to me."* Drop the match in the water.

GYPSY WITCH PRESENTS:
TROPICAL SPELLS HOODOOS & VOODOOS

Now say: "*In the name of the Holy Spirit, (name of lover) I bid you come to me.*" Drop match.

Read Psalm 40 in a whisper and envision your lover. Ask St. Expedite for speedier results for this spell. Do this each morning at 4:00AM. Your lover should speak to you before the 27th day.

To Rid Yourself of a Troublesome Neighbor

First, light a black candle and dress with castor oil. Write the neighbor's name on a piece of paper and the word "goodbye."

Place the paper under the candle. Now, mix powdered mud daubers nest with graveyard dirt and throw it at the neighbor's front door.

Recite Psalms 74, 101, and 109 three times each and let the candle burn out.

To Be Successful in Business

You will need 2 bottles of "Glory Water."

Dampen a green rag with "Glory Water" and wipe around the cash register or wherever you keep the money for making change for the public.

Wipe the tables, counter, desk, chairs, or whatever is used by the public. While wiping pray the Psalm 1, read the whole chapter.

Spray the place of business three times a week with "Glory Water" for 6 weeks.

GYPSY WITCH PRESENTS: TROPICAL SPELLS HOODOOS & VOODOOS

Psalm 5 for Court Case

If you have a court case or legal business in which you need to obtain the favor of a Judge or a panel or jury that will hear your case, you may use this candle spell using Psalm 5 to petition to the Saints and Angels that those who must make this judgment on you will be sympathetic to your plight.

Rise early in the morning for the three days prior to and including the morning of your court date while the sun is rising and pray Psalm 5. Pray the same Psalm 5 every night for the two days prior to your court date at sunset. Do this in front of a brown Court Case Candle, or a brown Indian Tobacco Spirit candle.

To prepare you will need a white ceramic dinner plate, some loose tobacco, 1 brown Court Case Candle or Indian Tobacco Spirit Candle, a copy of Summons to Court, lemon juice or Florida Water.

On the first day of this 3-day candle spell, make sure you have a copy of your Summons to Court, in which you have written across the back of the copy (do not use the original) this prayer:

Be merciful unto me, for the sake of Thy great, adorable and holy name, Chananjah, turn the heart of my Prince to me, and grant that He may regard me with Grace.

Sign the full name and birth date of the one going to court under this prayer. Clean candle with lemon juice or Florida Water. Spread loose tobacco lightly over petition paper on place. Place cleaned candle on top of paper and tobacco. Light candle and begin to pray Psalm 5.

If you are not guilty, you will be found innocent of the charge. If guilty, your sentence will be lessoned.

GYPSY WITCH PRESENTS:
TROPICAL SPELLS HOODOOS & VOODOOS

Uncrossing and Jinx Removing

You will need one 7-day glass white candle or a glass Uncrossing candle or a glass Jinx Removing candle, Double Strength Uncrossing or Jinx Removing Bath Crystals, saltpeter, 1 bottle Oil of Rosemary, 1 bottle of Uncrossing or Jinx Removing Condition Oil, 1 packet John the Conqueror Incense, 1 packet Church Charcoal.

Put two tablespoons of the Uncrossing or Jinx Removing Bath salts in the tub with one tablespoonful of saltpeter into your bath water while the water is running, make your wish to remove all envy, jealously and evil from you and repeat Psalm 11.

After your bath, anoint the palms of your hands and the bottoms of your feet with Uncrossing or Jinx Removing Condition Oil. Then, on a piece of parchment paper write your name nine times and place it under the Uncrossing or Jinx Removing Candle.

Place a bowl of water in which you have put three drops of Rosemary Oil next to the Uncrossing or Jinx Removing Candle.

Light candle and let it burn continuously until the crossed condition is removed, burning more than one candle after another until things have eased up.

When you go to light the second and subsequent candles, try to use a broom straw and "transfer the light" from the first or the currently lit candle to the unlit candle's wick. This makes a "perpetual light" that has not been blown out or gone out on its own.

If candle goes out before it has finished burning, start over from the beginning, as you have not done the spell properly or your intended victim knows that you are attempting to ward him off and is working against you stronger than before.

Each morning during this candle spell, burn the John the

GYPSY WITCH PRESENTS:
TROPICAL SPELLS HOODOOS & VOODOOS

Conqueror Incense on a church charcoal and read Psalm 69 to cast out any evil before leaving your home.

Vindication Spell

For this spell, you use a white 7-day novena type vigil candle in glass with your name under it and a black candle in glass with your enemies name under it. The candle colors represent complete destruction for your enemy and purity and cleanliness for you.

If you cannot find a black candle, use a white one for your enemy as well; just label each candle clearly so that you use the appropriate oil on the right candle.

Clean the candles with lemon juice and use Blessing Condition Oil on the white candle and use Revenge Condition Oil on the black candle.

Light both candles and read out loud Psalm 109 Prayer for Vindication and Vengeance.

Find Out the Name or Names of Thieves

For this spell you will need 2 bottles of Holy Water, 1 Compelling Power Incense, 1 Compelling Power Oil.

Pour one bottle of Holy Water on your front steps at sunrise, and one after the sun goes down. The same night, burn one whole box of Compelling Power Incense, pour the Compelling Power Oil on the incense slowly. While you are applying the oil, read Psalm 16 three times.

Defense and Protection Spell

You will need 4 or more railroad spikes, one half yard of red cloth, 4 or more containers of Red Devil Lye, 1 large bottle of

GYPSY WITCH PRESENTS:
TROPICAL SPELLS HOODOOS & VOODOOS

whiskey or rum, tobacco, Fiery Wall of Protection Incense, 4 or more Sixth Pentacles of Mars from the Key of Solomon or a protection talisman of your personal choice, glue, John the Conqueror Root Chips, Devil's Dung, red pepper.

This defense and protection ritual will be positioned at the four corners of your house. Perform during the hours of Mars if possible.

Soak the railroad spikes overnight in whiskey or rum; this will clean and feed the iron. Take spikes from rum and allow to air dry.

Cut the red cloth into 6 inch strips about one inch wide. If you only have four spikes, you will only need four strips of cloth. Set the strips aside.

Print out the talismans using the appropriate color ink. For the Sixth Pentacle of Mars, red is the appropriate color. Glue one talisman to each railroad spike. As you prepare your spikes, read Psalm 27 for protection.

Next tie a strip of red cloth around each railroad spike directly under the head of the spike. Now you will smoke the spikes in the Fiery Wall of Protection incense. Add some tobacco to heighten the effect.

As you wave each spike through the smoke of the incense, continue repeating your prayers and incantations. See the energy of your enemies repelled by a giant invisible force field surrounding your residence. Visualize your spiritual helpers forming an impenetrable perimeter of protection. You may wish to add red pepper or High John the Conqueror Root Chips to the Fiery Wall of Protection. You can also substitute Devils Dung for the High John or use the Devil's Dung alone as incense. All are effective alone or combined for protection work.

The next step is optional but effective. Prick your finger to draw blood and place a drop of your blood on each spike. If

GYPSY WITCH PRESENTS:
TROPICAL SPELLS HOODOOS & VOODOOS

pricking your finger is out of the question, dress the spikes with a little of your urine.

Now it is time to put your protection in place. Dig a hole at the four corners of your house and place a container of Red Devil Lye with the Devil facing outward in the hole. Cover the hole and drive the railroad spike into the ground next to the hole.

The head of the spikes should be flush with the ground and hopefully you will be able to locate it each month to feed the spike a shot glass of rum or whiskey mixed with some of your urine.

After you drive the railroad spike into the ground, pour a shot glass of whiskey on it and whisper Psalm 27.

Once a month, during the Full Moon or New Moon, feed the spikes in this manner.

Receive a Blessing Through a Dream

You will need Lucky Dream Incense and a bottle of Double Luck Perfume Oil.

Anoint yourself with Double Luck Perfume Oil, especially about the head. Burn Lucky Dream Incense. While the incense is burning, read the Psalm 57. Also ask that you may dream a lucky blessing dream this same night.

Stop Others from Having an Affair with Your Spouse or Lover

You will need 1 Strong Love Cologne, 7 bottles of Love Drawing Power Bath.

Write the 37th Psalm on a white piece of writing paper so that there are no spaces between the words and as one long

GYPSY WITCH PRESENTS:
TROPICAL SPELLS HOODOOS & VOODOOS

sentence. Hide it where no one can find it.

Take 7 baths using 1 bottle of Love Drawing Bath Oil for each bath.

Use the Strong Love Cologne when you are in your love one's company.

How to Compel Your Loved One to Return to You

Needed for this spell: 2 Love Drawing Power Bath, 1 bottle Strong Love Cologne.

Read the 4th Psalm for 9 days.

Take 7 baths with Love Drawing Bath.

After each bath, anoint your chest with a few drops of Strong Love Cologne.

How to Remove Evil

Required for this spell: 3 bottles of Stop Evil Floor Wash, 3 Jars of Commanding Pepper.

Wash your floors with the Stop Evil Floor Wash.

Empty the Commanding Pepper in a paper bag and read the Psalm 37 over it once a day for 3 days.

Carry the bag to a body of water and throw it into the water.

Psalm Money Spell

Use a yellow glass encased candle and pray the 23rd Psalm over it 7 times.

GYPSY WITCH PRESENTS: TROPICAL SPELLS HOODOOS & VOODOOS

State and pray for your specific needs and requests.

Place the candle somewhere safe and allow it to burn out by itself.

Archangel Michael Protection

Light a Michael Archangel novena candle, or Holy candle with Saint Michael the archangel Holy card leaning on it.
Now dress it with some orange oil and say this prayer:

Great Archangel Michael Archangel, defend us in battle, be our defense against the wickedness and snares of the devil.

May God rebuke our enemies, we humbly pray; and do thou, O Prince of the heavenly host, by the power of God, thrust into Hell the Adversary and all other evil spirits who prowl about the world for the ruin of souls.

Amen.

Then recite, or read Psalm 91 and after the candle burns out you will be protected from evil.

Hoodoo Money Spell

Materials needed: small black cotton bag, a silver dime, a nickel, and a penny, dirt from crossroads, red brick dust (made by crushing a brick), water from a river, sunlight, a piece of green string.

Begin reciting the single verse of Psalm 15:5. You will continue repeating this over and over until all of the materials are in the bag.

Place the nickel in the bag, then place the dirt in the bag, then the dime, then the brick dust, then the penny.

GYPSY WITCH PRESENTS:
TROPICAL SPELLS HOODOOS & VOODOOS

Tie up the top of the bag so nothing can get out with a piece of green string.

Immerse the bag in the river water and begin reciting Psalm 15:5 again. Hold it under and keep reciting Psalm 15:5 for twenty seconds before taking it back out.

Let the bag dry out in the sunlight. Make sure it is completely dry.

Sleep with the bag under your bed until the money comes.

Psalm 37 as a Cleansing Ritual

Light two small white offertory candles and stand between them. Wash with clear rain water, spring water, or tap water to which tears have been added while reciting the Psalm.

Burn 7-11 Holy Type, or Blessing, or Frankincense Resin incense while reciting the Psalm.

Change Your Luck Spell

Get out of bed before sunrise on any day and, facing east, repeat the following prayer, which contains the holy name *Jiheje*, or "he is and will be":

> *May it please thee,*
> *O holy Jiheje,*
> *To bring prosperity to my travels and endeavors.*
> *For the sake of thy great name,*
> *Grant that my wishes and desires be fulfilled.*
> *Amen.*

Now, thinking of *Jiheje*, read Psalm 4 three times. Contemplate the sunrise, and afterward go about your day with confidence and peace.

GYPSY WITCH PRESENTS: TROPICAL SPELLS HOODOOS & VOODOOS

Simple Wish Spell

Take a blank piece of paper and write whatever you want to take place in large letters.

Burn the paper over a bowl/cauldron, while visualizing the wish that you want.

Take the ashes outside and toss into the wind. Then say Psalm 4 out loud.

Your wish will soon be granted.

GYPSY WITCH PRESENTS:
TROPICAL SPELLS HOODOOS & VOODOOS

From Hoodoo Curio Catalog, King Novelty Co. 1944

GYPSY WITCH PRESENTS:
TROPICAL SPELLS HOODOOS & VOODOOS

PART SIX
How to Make a Mojo/Gris Gris Bag

If you want to protect yourself and ward off evil or harm that is being done to you, you can make a Mojo/Gris Gris bag. Mojo bags are carried in the form of a doll or a bag and are essentially a means of carrying a charm or a spell. These can be carried or worn. If you are women, then hold or wear it on your left side. If you are a man, than carry or wear it on your right side. Making a Mojo bag is very simple. They can be used for protection and to focus and meditate on a problem.

Traditionally, a Mojo bag is a two inch by three inch drawstring bag into which special herbs, stones, personal effects, roots, bones, coins, metal lucky charms, crystals, good luck tokens, carved stones, and European seals and sigils that have been written on parchment paper. You can either buy a bag made from velvet, satin, hemp or any other material, or you can also make one out of any material you like.

The color of your Mojo bag depends on what you are using it for. The most common covering for a Mojo bag is red flannel, because red is considered a lucky color for a large number of life's conditions. Other colors include: green (for money), blue (for peacefulness), or white (for blessings and safety), purple (for spirituality), black (for pain/relief/repelling), white (for positive energy). Also, never decorate the outside of a Mojo bag. They are supposed to be kept simple.

Making a Mojo will add more of your personal energies to it. Simply cut out a square piece of cloth that will be large enough to hold 13 small items.

You can choose items as dirt, soil, rocks, plants, herbs or anything else that is in relation to yourself or your situation. Such as, if the Mojo bag is for protection then choosing items that symbolize protection is best. Or if the bag is to return a lost love or resolve a love conflict, then choose items that represent love or that person or both. However, you can only add 13 items, no more than that.

Once you have picked your items, place them in the bag or on the material that you are using for the bag. Place them all in there. It is okay if they are on top of each other and

GYPSY WITCH PRESENTS:
TROPICAL SPELLS HOODOOS & VOODOOS

fall over, you will be caring the bag with you.

When adding the items chant or speak your intentions and desires. Once all the items have been added, use a piece of string or cord to tie the bag closed. Make sure that you can wrap it around the top of the bag a few times so that none of the items will fall out and you can tie it securely.

Once you have your Mojo bag, you should keep it out of sight – and especially out of the range of touch – of others. A Mojo bag is typically worn by a person under the clothes, for it is said that if someone touches your Mojo bag, its luckiness will be "killed." When you are not carrying your conjure bag, you can keep it hidden away somewhere safe.

In many cases, when you have finished your Mojo bag you will need to personalize it – that is, you will need to add an appropriate personal concern to the bag, dress it with oil, whisky, Hoyt's Cologne, or another appropriate liquid, and smoke it in incense.

Feeding the bag – dabbing it with liquid and in smoke, speaking to it, and praying over it – is a ritual that most folks do on their bags once a week to keep them working.

That's all there is to it. Carry your bag with you or pin it to yourself. Use it when you need to focus on your problem or situation whenever necessary.

Powerful Prosperity Mojo Bag

To make a powerful prosperity Mojo bag, obtain a rue plant and a vervain plant from a local nursery. Make a small pouch of bright red velvet, cotton, or silk. In this red bag put coarse salt. Stitch the pouch closed. Then, form a larger red bag with a drawstring of red cord. Into this bag loosely place the little pouch containing the salt, some rue leaves and some veravin.

This bag will bring you both prosperity and protection.

Mojo Bag for Anger Management

In a black sachet, add a Hematite and the following herbs:

GYPSY WITCH PRESENTS: TROPICAL SPELLS HOODOOS & VOODOOS

Amaranths, Pansy and Wild Violet.

Mojo Bag for Control and Dominance

In a purple sachet include a Lapis Lazuli as many of the following herbs as possible: Dragons Blood, Yellow Gentian, American Sweet Gum, Iron Weed, Jalap Bindweed, Joe Pye Weed, Licorice, Mango, Masterwort, Primrose, Quassia and Sweet Sedge.

Mojo Bag for Courage

In a blue sachet include an Amazonite and as many of the following herbs as possible (not to exceed 13): Be-Still, Borage, Black Cohosh and Echinacea.

Mojo Bag for Fascination

In a pink sachet, add a magnet, a small sea shell, a small key and two sewing needles bound by red fabric.

Mojo Bag for Fertility

In a green sachet include egg shells and the following herbs: Queens Delight, Motherwort and Raspberry.

Mojo Bag to Find a Job

In a brown sachet include as many of the following herbs as possible (not to exceed 13): Devil's Shoestring, Gravelroot, Guelder Rose, Heartsease and Kava.

GYPSY WITCH PRESENTS: TROPICAL SPELLS HOODOOS & VOODOOS

Mojo Bag to Find a Mistress

In a red sachet include the following herbs: Cardamom and Ginger.

Mojo Bag to Heal Broken Heart

Include in a blue sachet a sewing needle, a Rose Quartz gemstone and as many of the following herbs as possible (not to exceed 13): Amaranths, Balm of Gilead, Woody Nightshade and Violet.

Mojo Bag for Fidelity

In a red sachet, include a link from a dog chain, a Ruby and the following herbs: Caraway, Coriander and Ivy.

Mojo Bag for Justice

In a brown sachet add the image of Themis, the Greek goddess of justice, a Bloodstone, and these herbs: Carnation, Cascara Sagrada and Skunk Cabbage.

Mojo Bag for Love (Attract)

In a red or pink sachet, place a small wax heart, a Rose Quartz gemstone and the following herbs: Clover, Feverfew, Heartsease, Iris, Mandrake, Passion Flower, Rose and Senna.

Mojo Bag to Return Past Lover

Include in a purple sachet a magnet, a small wax heart, a lady bug and the herbs: Forget-Me-Not and Loosestrife.

GYPSY WITCH PRESENTS: TROPICAL SPELLS HOODOOS & VOODOOS

Mojo Bag for Vigor

In a red sachet, include Amber and the following herbs as possible: Star Anise, Horse Chestnut, Juniper, Sarsaparilla and Saw Palmetto.

Mojo Bag for Luck (In Court)

In a brown sachet add the image of Themis, the Greek goddess of justice, a Bloodstone, and the following herbs: Buckthorn, Cinquefoil, Heartsease, Lily of the Valley, Oregano, Skunk Cabbage, Sumac and Tansy.

Mojo Bag for Luck (In Gambling)

In a green sachet add Aventurine, a seven-sided dice and the following herbs: Arrowroot, Comfrey, Devil's Shoestring, Guelder Rose and Orchid.

Mojo Bag for Protection (For a Car)

Add a Tigers Eye gemstone and the following herbs: Angelica and Plantain.

Mojo Bag for Protection (From Disease)

In a black sachet, include an Onyx, the image of a snake and the following herbs: Anemone and Posey.

Mojo Bag for Protection (From Harassment)

In a black sachet, include an Sapphire and the following herbs: Balmony and Black Cohosh.

GYPSY WITCH PRESENTS:
TROPICAL SPELLS HOODOOS & VOODOOS

Mojo Bag for Protection (From Jealousy)

In a black sachet, include a Peridot and the following herbs: Dogwood, Plantain and Squaw Vine.

Mojo Bag for Protection (From Weapons)

In a black sachet, add an Agate and the following herbs: Amaranths, Edelweiss and Heather.

Mojo Bag for Joy and Luck

You will need two small equal pieces of red cloth, red woolen thread, a crumb of bread, a pinch of salt, and a teaspoon of rue.

Sew three sides of the four sides of red cloth together with the red woolen thread. Turn the bag outside in because it should have been inside out when you were sewing it.

Put the crumb of bread, the pinch of salt, and the teaspoon of rue in it and sew it up.

Say this Chant for good fortune:

This bag I sew for luck for me, and also for my family, That it may keep by night and day, troubles and illness far away.

Hang the bag over your bed, your window, or keep it in your purse.

Mojo Bag to Attract a Lover

You will need 5 Cardamom seeds, 1 small key, 1 Queen Elizabeth Root, 5 strands of pubic hair, magnetic sand, a lodestone.

GYPSY WITCH PRESENTS: TROPICAL SPELLS HOODOOS & VOODOOS

Gather all of the ingredients and light a pink candle, and some sweet smelling incense.

On a scrap of paper, write the qualities that you are seeking in a lover, turn the paper 90 degrees and write your name across your description nine times.

Place the lodestone on top of the paper; sprinkle it with magnetic sand and your pubic hairs.

Wrap the paper around the lodestone tightly so that the magnetic sand and hairs cannot fall out. Place the lodestone in the Mojo bag along with all the other ingredients, tie the bag securely, and smoke it in incense while focusing on your goal.

Mojo Bag for Psychic Ability

You will need Celery Seed, Anise Seed, Althea, Acacia, Poppy Flowers, Calendula, and Star Anise.

Mix Celery Seed, Anise Seed, Althea Leaves, Acacia, Poppy Flowers, Calendula, and Star Anise in a muslin bag and keep it beneath your pillow where you sleep.

Mojo Bag for Gambling Luck

You will need 1 Buckeye, Silver Dime, Pair of Dice, Rabbit's Foot, Cinnamon, Allspice, and Chamomile

Place a Buckeye nut in a green flannel bag with a Silver Dime, a pair of dice, and a Rabbit's Foot, plus three money-luck herbs such as Cinnamon, Allspice, and Chamomile. Dress the bag with Money Drawing Oil and Hoyt's Cologne.

Mojo Bag for Protection

You will need 1 Whole Devil's Bit, 9 pieces Devil's Shoe String

GYPSY WITCH PRESENTS:
TROPICAL SPELLS HOODOOS & VOODOOS

Roots, 1 Devil's Pod, and 1 Pinch Devil's Dung.

Combine a whole Devil's Bit root, nine pieces of Devil's Shoe String Roots, and a Devil Pod in a black leather bag.

On a small piece of paper, write the name of the person from whom you want to protect yourself, cross and cover the name with your name, written three times, and fold the name paper around a pinch of Devil's Dung, folding away from you each time until it is a small packet.

Dress the packet with Run Devil Run Oil and place it in the bag. This is among the strongest reversing hands that can be made, but you may have to find and dig your own Devil's Bit, or grow it in your own garden, for the whole root is not always available commercially.

Mojo Bag for Quick Sex

For this Mojo bag you will need armpit hair, pubic hair, toenail clippings, 1 teaspoon Coriander Seeds, Lemon Grass, 1 Cinnamon stick, and 1 High John the Conqueror Root.

Light a red candle and some incense. Char the end of the Cinnamon Stick and draw the symbol for Mars on a scrap of paper.

Write your name inside the circular part of the symbol and wrap the paper around the Cinnamon stick, securing it with red thread.

Place the cinnamon stick in a red Mojo bag along with your personal concerns, coriander seeds, lemon grass, and finally a High John the Conqueror Root.

Mojo Bag for Love

You will need 2 matched lodestones, magnetic sand, Queen

GYPSY WITCH PRESENTS: TROPICAL SPELLS HOODOOS & VOODOOS

Elizabeth Root, John the Conqueror Root, Cherry bark, Lavender, Red Clover, Damiana, and Catnip.

Write the name of the individual that you desire on paper nine times, cross and cover this with your own name also nine times. Place the matched Lodestones on the paper, and sprinkle it with magnetic sand. Wrap the paper around the Lodestones and place these in a red Mojo bag along with the other ingredients.

Anoint the Mojo bag with Love Me, or Come to Me Oil.

Mojo Bag for Prosperity

For this bag you will need 1 strand Conjuror's Hair, finger nail clippings, earth from near a bank, 5 dried Bay leaves, 1 penny, 1 nickel, 1 dime, and 1 quarter.

Into a small green drawstring bag place a lock of your hair, fingernail clippings, dirt from around a bank, five dried bay leaves, a penny, a nickel, a quarter, and a dime.

Tie the bag securely and bury it for 5 days near a bank or any thriving business (as the moon grows).

Anoint the Mojo bag with Money Drawing Oil and carry it in your pocket or purse.

Mojo Bag for Legal Troubles

You will need Calendula, Anise Seeds, Deer's Tongue, Celery Seed, Tobacco Snuff, Cascara Sagrada, Dill Seed, and Little John.

Write the names of those who oppose you on a piece of brown grocery bag paper and cross their names with your own three times.

GYPSY WITCH PRESENTS:
TROPICAL SPELLS HOODOOS & VOODOOS

Wrap a pinch each of Calendula, Anise Seeds, Deer's Tongue, Celery Seed, Tobacco Snuff, Cascara Sagrada, and Dill seed in the name paper, folding it away from you saying: *"May this trouble be removed from me."*

Tie the packet with thread and carry it in your pocket when you go to court. In the courtroom, chew a bit of Little John Root and spit it onto the paper wrapped Mojo.

GYPSY WITCH PRESENTS:
TROPICAL SPELLS HOODOOS & VOODOOS

From Hoodoo Curio Catalog, King Novelty Co. 1944

GYPSY WITCH PRESENTS: TROPICAL SPELLS HOODOOS & VOODOOS

PART SEVEN
Hoodoo Rootworking

The use of herbs for hoodoo conjuring has been a part of hoodoo practice for as far back as oral histories and written records exist. It is very likely that their use combines African traditions of healing, Native American plant lore, and information taken from medieval European herbal grimores.

Herbal preparations are used in a number of different ways by hoodoo rootworkers and plant species often gain their reputation for magickally influencing situations through the Doctrine of Signatures, which says that the appearance of a natural curio points the way toward its use in magick.

Hoodoo formulas like Love Me, Crown of Success, and Van Van are based in specific leaves, roots, and flowers and the magickal properties given to them are through decades of experience and tradition. Herbs that are home grown can be harvested at specific times and prayed over both prior to and after harvesting has taken place.

The leaves, roots, stems, seeds, and flowers of magickal plants are usually dried after harvesting, and that way they may be used in many different forms of hoodoo magick such as oils, Mojo bags, candles, incense, etc.

Here is a list of some of the popular herbs that are traditionally used in hoodoo rootwork.

African Dream Root or Silene capensis: This obscure flowering species is regarded by shamans of the South African region as a type of medicinal root that they call "Undela Ziimhlophe," which translates literally as "white paths" or white ways." It was said that when drank with something of the person's (hair, sweat, etc.), it allows that person to dream-walk or walk around in another person's dreams.

Agrimony: Powerful defensive herb that not only can prevent hexes and banish evil spirits, but often will reverse the effects of a spell onto the caster. In addition, agrimony can be used in a potion to induce a deep sleep almost indistinguishable from death.

GYPSY WITCH PRESENTS: TROPICAL SPELLS HOODOOS & VOODOOS

Alfalfa: Traditionally used in combination with other herbs to bring good fortune. Not extremely powerful on its own, but very useful when added to charms against poverty or bad luck. Alfalfa is sometimes burned and the ashes scattered around the outside of a house against poverty and hunger.

Allspice: Like alfalfa, more of a catalyst than an individual power. It's often used as an element of charms involving money and luck. Allspice has an interesting association with creativity and in some traditions is used to spark ideas or artistic inspiration.

Altamisa: This makes a very good love and attraction bath.

Amaranth: Known for its protective abilities and for use in calling spirits. A whole amaranth plant, uprooted under a full moon and then worn under the shirt, is a powerful protection against physical attacks. The dried flowers are useful in calling the dead.

Angelica: Also known as "archangel," angelica root is very powerful in protective functions. Sprinkled in the four corners of a house, it protects against evil, and it is a powerful talisman when carried on a person. Used at the beginning and ending of rituals, it has a strong blessing effect. Also associated with good luck, particularly in certain Native American traditions, where it was used to bring fortune in gambling. Smoking the leaves can cause visions.

Anise: Raises vibrations to the highest possible psychic level. Good for bringing about changes in attitude (refocusing), and for astral travel, dreams, crystal gazing, and meditation. In a pillow, it is said to keep away nightmares. For any type of clairvoyance or divination or mental exercises.

Anisette (liquor): Is used during voodoo initiations to anoint the head.

Anointing oil: The biblical traditions of anointing with oil stems

GYPSY WITCH PRESENTS:
TROPICAL SPELLS HOODOOS & VOODOOS

from a specific oil mentioned in Exodus 30, which was composed of cinnamon, calamus, cassia, and myrrh, infused in olive oil. This oil is an important element in the performance of certain protective rituals.

Arrow Root: Mix with gambling powder to increase luck.

Asafetida: Also known as devil's dung or stinking gum for its odor, asafetida is a very powerful protectant. When burned, it will drive away evil and dispel spirits. It can be used in various rituals of exorcism. It is also said to attract wolves.

Balm of Gilead: Also known as balsam of Mecca. A resinous gum extracted from the balsam poplar tree. Known for its protective and healing properties since biblical times.

Barberry: A dangerous herb that is more suited to dark magick than positive uses. When sprinkled around a house, will provoke argument and bitterness. This effect can be reversed if barberry is combined with bay leaves and vetivert, but this forces the herb to operate against its nature and is a tricky undertaking.

Basil: Used in a wide variety of rituals and sachets to purify, protect, and increase harmony and well-being. If sprinkled over a sleeping lover, it will ensure both fidelity and sexual interest. Ubiquitous in spells of love and prosperity. Basil can be burned as incense in certain exorcism rituals and when sprinkled on the floor provides some protection against the physical presence of evil.

Bay: The visions of the Delphic oracle are said to have been the product of chewing bay leaves. They will also induce visions when burned and when placed under the pillow can bring prophetic dreams. In potions, bay leaves can bring a kind of clairvoyance, and when the leaves are kept on the person, they will protect against evil—although in some traditions this is reversed, and the bay's power is said to be in its use for hexing others.

GYPSY WITCH PRESENTS: TROPICAL SPELLS HOODOOS & VOODOOS

Bayberry: Traditionally used in the manufacture of candles, bayberry works as a powerful catalyst for the magical properties of other herbs—usually in a negative direction. Can be used to cause depression and to force the collection of debts. Also can be used to attract a male lover, though the bayberry's magical complexion makes the wisdom of such a romance questionable.

Belladonna: Apart from its use in optometry to dilate pupils, belladonna has a number of magical properties. It is extremely dangerous to use, being toxic in any but the tiniest amounts. Carefully employed, however, it can be used to facilitate bilocation and astral projection, as well as visionary states. Belladonna is often used in funeral rituals to ease the passage of the soul between worlds. It is also known as nightshade, and some folklore suggests that application of belladonna can prevent someone bitten by a werewolf from becoming one.

Berry of The Fish: Sprinkle in enemies yard to make them move away or keep away from you.

Beth Root: Attract a mate by secretly mixing this into food or drink.

Benzoin: Another herb whose primary use is as an intensifier. Particularly noted for its combination with cinnamon'; when burned together, these herbs bring material success. Very dangerous if used to increase the power of a hex or negative spell. Mixed and burned with dittany of Crete, sandalwood, and vanilla, benzoin forms a powerful aid to astral projection.

Bergamot: The leaves, if rubbed on money, will ensure wise spending. If placed in the wallet, they are said to attract money. Bergamot is also reputed to enhance intuition and can be used in various combinations to induce prophetic dreams.

Betony: Druidic rituals employed betony in several capacities. At midsummer, it was added to bonfires, and those who jumped through the smoke would be purified of malevolent influences. Dried and placed inside a pillow, it ensures restful sleep and wards off nightmares.

GYPSY WITCH PRESENTS:
TROPICAL SPELLS HOODOOS & VOODOOS

Bindweed: Useful in both protective and aggressive magic, bindweed overwhelms the intentions of its target. Depending on the other herbs in the charm, it can be employed to control another person or simply thwart his intentions. Not to be taken internally, since it is a powerful laxative and purgative.

Bistort: When used in conjunction with juniper and allspice, bistort will draw money. It is also used to help couples conceive a child.

Bittersweet: Toss into an enemy's path or yard to make them leave town and never look back.

Black Candle Tobacco: Mix with salt and burn with a black candle, said to win most court cases.

Blackberry: The blackberry is a powerful protective plant. It is often used as part of a wreath, in combination with ivy and rowan, which when placed at the door will ward off evil. A blackberry bramble that grows in a natural arch is said to be both a gateway to the fairy realm and a strong healing location. If crawled through both backward and forward, the arch will cure numerous bodily ailments.

Black Cohosh: Make into a tea and add to bath water, it is said to ensure a long and happy life.

Black Mustard Seed: Causes problems and disturbances when sprinkled in an enemies yard.

Black snakeroot: When used by a man, black snakeroot can be a powerful charm to create or destroy love. If burned with objects related to an individual, the root exerts a powerful repelling influence on that person; its opposite function is to compel love when burned with Adam and Eve root.

Bladderwrack: Carry while traveling for protection, said to cause confusion if placed by stall of enemies.

GYPSY WITCH PRESENTS: TROPICAL SPELLS HOODOOS & VOODOOS

Blood root: A favorite voodoo root used for defeating hexes and spells aimed to harm you.

Blue Flag: Mix with money drawing incense for financial gain.

Blueberry: Whether eaten or used as a charm or sachet, blueberry is an extremely potent protection against treachery and deception. Eating blueberries increases an individual's ability to resist psychic influence or assault. Placed near the door of a household, it will keep unwanted visitors away.

Boldo Leaves: Sprinkle around the house to ward off evil. Must be renewed once a month.

Boneset: To curse an enemy, burn as incense along with a black candle inscribed with their name.

Broom Tops: Make into a tea and sprinkle around the home to clear away all evil.

Buchu leaves: Native to southern Africa, buchu has been incorporated into various New World divination rituals. Burned with frankincense, buchu can bring prophetic dreams; taken as an infusion it can strengthen powers of clairvoyance.

Burdock: In the Middle Ages, knights often rode into battle with a sprig of burdock, which was said to protect and promote healing, particularly of the feet. A charm of burdock root, gathered under a waning moon and strung around the neck, will ward away evil influences.

Cacao: Considered food of the gods by the Aztecs and often used in potions and charms to gain love or throw off malign influences. It is also used to quiet angry or restless spirits and is a standard element of Latin American séances.

Calamus: Often used as a binding element in charms or spells, calamus can also be used by itself to control an individual. Grown in a garden, it will bring luck to the gardener and enhance the yield of the plants close to it.

GYPSY WITCH PRESENTS: TROPICAL SPELLS HOODOOS & VOODOOS

Calendula: More familiarly known as the marigold, calendula is used in a variety of ways. In certain rituals, it is said to give knowledge of the language of birds. Burned as incense, the petals consecrate objects intended for use in divinatory rituals. Another use of the marigold is in rituals to attain a clairvoyant state or to communicate with supernatural beings.

Camphor: Often used as part of cleansing rituals, camphor is also frequently used in charms to end unwanted romantic entanglements or lessen desire.

Caraway: Said to be a potent protective herb, especially against Lilith and malign spirits of a sexual nature. Also frequently used in spells and charms designed to beguile a lover. A parallel tradition holds that any object—for example, a wallet or purse—containing caraway seeds cannot be stolen.

Cardamom: Although it is sometimes said to have powerful properties of its own where loves and lust are concerned, cardamom is most often used to catalyze the effects of other herbs in sexual or love spells.

Carob: The pods of this plant are often used as a part of charms to attract wealth, but carob's more esoteric uses include burning as incense to repel poltergeists or—when used by a witch—to attract a familiar.

Catnip: Once chewed by warriors before battle to increase their ferocity, catnip is used to aid in the creation of the bond between a witch and a cat familiar and is generally known to increase the intensity of psychic abilities. Also, the leaves can be dried and burned as part of love/sex rituals.

Cayenne: One of the more powerful catalysts in the herbal repertoire, especially as part of spells intended to control, cayenne is equally useful in creating or breaking hexes. It is also a strong ingredient in counter spells and can reverse the effects of a negative spell on the caster.

Cedar: The smoke of the cedar is a common ingredient in

GYPSY WITCH PRESENTS: TROPICAL SPELLS HOODOOS & VOODOOS

psychic rituals and is also used to prevent nightmares.

Chamomile: Traditionally used to protect from the evil eye or to break curses, chamomile is a gentle yet powerful agent in various love and prosperity rituals. Often it is used to prepare the mind and body for magic, due to its calming and centering properties.

Chewing John Root: Chewing the root and throwing it away sends back a curse, use for court cases.

Cinnamon: A powerful part of spells designed for psychic power or control, cinnamon is especially protective when burned in a mixture of sandalwood, frankincense, and myrrh. It is a common ingredient in spells or charms intended to capture male love or lust.

Clove: Often used to add force to a hex, cloves are powerful catalysts in spells of exorcism and purification. Also they are worn or carried to offer protection from evil spirits and in many traditions is strung over cribs to protect infants.

Clover: Generally used as a ward against evil and bad fortune, clover is also an important element in rituals of clairvoyance. Holding a four-leaf clover conveys the power to see fairies and detect the presence of spirits.

Comfrey leaf: An important part of spells to protect travelers, comfrey leaf is also incorporated into rituals of spiritual projection.

Cubeb: A form of pepper native to Indonesia, cubeb was included in medieval rituals to repel demons, particularly the incubus. This antisexual property is reversed in hoodoo practice, which often uses the berries as part of love magic.

Cumin: Mixed with salt, cumin is part of a common household charm to repel evil and bad luck. It is also used as a binding influence in spells that require a lighter touch rather than pure magical force.

GYPSY WITCH PRESENTS:
TROPICAL SPELLS HOODOOS & VOODOOS

Damiana: Particularly in Latin American traditions that stem from Mayan and Aztec lore, damiana is used as an aphrodisiac and component in sex magic. It is also an important part of rituals to bring about visionary states.

Dandelion: Dried and used as tea, the roots and leaves of the dandelion call spirits and enhance psychic abilities. In Celtic paganism, Samhain rituals made use of dandelion for divination.

Devil Bone Root: Cut into small pieces and carry in a red flannel bag to ward off arthritis.

Devil Shoestring: Carry in a red flannel bag for protection or in pocket for drawing gambling luck.

Devil's Bit: Often substituted for low John, or galangal, in hoodoo magic, devil's bit adds compulsive and controlling power to whatever charm it is made part of, whether involving exorcism, love or protection.

Echinacea: Apart from its healing and protective properties, Echinacea was used in various Native American traditions as an offering to spirits, who would then strengthen the shaman's magic.

Elder: The leaves of the elder, gathered at the right time and place, prevent witches from entering a house. It is used in divination, but the tree's magic is ambivalent, since it is associated with witchcraft and walking under an elder can bring the attention of malign forces.

Elecampane: Named inula by the Greeks because of their belief that Helen of Troy carried a bunch of it away to Phrygia at her abduction by Paris, elecampane is a powerful element in love charms and also improves the potency of scrying rituals.

Fennel: Sacred in both the Anglo-Saxon and kabalistic traditions, fennel is part of meditative rituals and counter spells to remove hexes. In the Middle Ages, fennel was combined

GYPSY WITCH PRESENTS: TROPICAL SPELLS HOODOOS & VOODOOS

with St. John's wort in a midsummer ritual to prevent witchcraft and repel evil spirits. Somewhat unpredictable, fennel can prevent possession but also twist the function of other herbs and magical processes.

Fenugreek: The Egyptians buried fenugreek in the tombs of certain pharaohs, including Tutankhamen. It is associated with luck and success.

Fig: Sacred to Dionysus and Juno, among others, the fig was also used in rituals around the Celtic holiday Beltane. Also it is an important part of divination rituals in virtually every culture where it is known.

Five Finger Grass: Also known as cinquefoil, this herb is useful in protecting against hexes, but when mixed with soot its influence reverses, and it becomes a potent hexing agent itself.

Frankincense: Used as a divinatory offering across times and cultures, frankincense is part of numerous exorcism and protection rituals as well. Often it provides a stable base around which other elements are combined into incense. When burned in conjunction with myrrh—the feminine counterpart to its masculine association—frankincense provides a balancing influence on charms and rituals.

Galangal: Also known as low John, this root is most useful in creating change where subtle and indirect means will be more successful than direct action. A tricky and somewhat devious herb, it is, when used properly, a powerful breaker of spells and protector of health. As part of hoodoo practice, it will bring money if placed in a leather sachet with silver.

Galbanum oil: The sixteenth-century grimoire *Liber Juratus* refers to this oil, a simple infusion of galbanum resin. According to the Juratus, it is used in rituals aiming to contact both angels and spirits.

Garlic: Long before it was used to ward off vampires, garlic was part of Greek ritual, being places on stone cairns at crossroads as a sacrifice to Hecate. An Islamic legend states

GYPSY WITCH PRESENTS:
TROPICAL SPELLS HOODOOS & VOODOOS

that garlic first grew out of the prints of Satan's left foot as he left the Garden of Eden. (Onions grew from the right.) Soldiers from Roman times through the medieval period ate garlic before battle to protect them and give them courage. Garlic hung over the door of a home not only wards away evil but prevents an envious person from entering. It is a powerful protective ingredient in the charms of most cultures.

Ginger: Eaten before the performance of magic, ginger increases the power of a charm. It is particularly effective catalyst in love spells and in some Pacific cultures is used by sailors to prevent illness and forestall the approach of bad weather.

Ginseng: The name derives from jinchen, meaning "like a man," a reference to the root's shape. Like other herbs noted for their resemblance to parts of the body, from mandrake to John the Conqueror—ginseng is used primarily in sexual and health magic, although it has also become part of rituals to break curses.

Goofer dust: A standard ingredient in hoodoo, goofer dust almost always has some graveyard dirt in it, but beyond that, the other ingredients depend on what kind of spell you want to use it in. dried and ground-up snake heads are another common ingredient. Sometimes lizard heads. Salt and pepper are also typical, especially if the goofer dust is supposed to protect rather than attack.

Graveyard dirt: Hoodoo spells both protective and offensive use graveyard dirt as a fundamental component. The manner of collection, and the ways in which the dirt is used, dictate the effect of the spell. A hostile spell requires the collection of dirt from someone who died badly or who while alive perhaps bore the intended victim ill will. A protective spell might use the dirt from the grave of someone beloved to the practitioner or person to be protected. Graveyard dirt must be paid for by an offering—usually a Mercury dime, to the spirit inhabiting the grave from which the dirt is to be dug.

GYPSY WITCH PRESENTS: TROPICAL SPELLS HOODOOS & VOODOOS

Gravel Root: Helps get a job, carry in green flannel bag and anoint with Job oil.

Hawthorn: Long used in the rituals of protection and purification, hawthorn symbolized marriage to the Romans. They also placed it in cribs to protect infants from evil spirits. The Greeks too considered it lucky, but it became identified with witchcraft in Europe and was considered unlucky for that reason—and also perhaps because of the belief that Christ's crown of thorns was made from hawthorn. In the British Isles, it is said that wherever oak, ash, and hawthorn grow together, fairies may be seen.

Hazel: In Celtic tradition, hazel is a tree of wisdom and inspiration. The branches are commonly used for diving rods or tied into a cross for protection or reconciliation. Hazelnuts are said to bring wisdom and visions.

Hemlock: Socrates' downfall, hemlock has the particular property of reversing the power of any mixture to which it is added. It is much more potent in negative spells than positive and a very strong aid to most hexes.

Hemp seed: Burned as an incense, hemp seed improves scrying and divination and will attract spirit guides. It is also useful in the making of magic candles.

Hibiscus: Useful as an aphrodisiac and in love spells. Also used to induce dreams and enhance psychic ability and divination.

Holly leaf: A powerful ritual plant, holly wards away misfortune and evil, including lightning. Magickal tools and implements made from its wood will be strengthened.

Holy Ghost Root: prolongs life and protects against evil spirits and witchcraft.

Holy Thistle: Brew into a tea and sprinkle around the house to get rid of a jinx thrown on you.

GYPSY WITCH PRESENTS: TROPICAL SPELLS HOODOOS & VOODOOS

Holy Water: Water which has been passed by a priest, or bishop for the purpose of baptism or for the blessing of persons, places or things.

Hops: Often used in tea to restore balance after the performance of magick.

Horehound: Called the "seed of Horus" by the ancient Egyptians, horehound is a strong protection against sorcery. Crushed and scattered during an exorcism ritual, it improves the prospects for success and can protect the exorcist.

Hyssop: Bathe in to keep away evil eye and ward of jinx and to purify.

Job Tears: Carry 7 for luck, and having one wish come true.

Joe Pie Weed: Carry in blue flannel bag to gain popularity and friendship, anoint with pure Orris oil.

Juniper: Used in Mediterranean traditions since prehistoric times, juniper has long associations with protection, exorcism, and (though later association with Jupiter) male sexual potency. A powerfully direct herb, not useful in subtler spells.

King of the Woods: A man carries for this control over his woman.

Knot Weed: Used to get rid of an enemy.

Ladies Thumb: Draws love to you.

Lucky Hand Root: Carried in red flannel bag with good luck charms while gambling for best of luck.

Lemongrass: A useful aid in the development of psychic powers, lemongrass also has powers in formulas designed to cause problems and bad luck in the target's life.

Licorice: Used by the Egyptians as an aphrodisiac, licorice root is still a common ingredient in strong and direct love and potency spells.

Lilac: A clarifying and peaceful herb, lilac assists clairvoyance and past-life awareness. In combinations and sachets, it ensures that the positive qualities of the other components outweigh the negative.

Lobelia: A poison that, like other poisons, must be used with great caution. Lobelia can turn a meddlesome or annoying charm lethal.

Lotus: Associated with Egyptian magic, and referred to in Greek and Indian traditions as well, the lotus is one of the most powerful gateways to astral awareness and mystical understanding.

Madjet oil: Known from an inscription on the Temple of Horus at Edfu, this oil was intended to reconstitute the bodies of the dead in the afterlife. Its primary ingredients are cinnamon, myrrh, pine resin, and lemongrass. Historically applied to the statue of the god, it is also useful in various rituals involving contact with the dead.

Mandrake root: Because of its humanoid shape, the mandrake root has long been a powerful element in the spells of all sorts. Used in alchemical rites create homunculi, it has also been used in image magic to stand in for the human target. Tea made from the mandrake has enormous visionary power. A whole mandrake root is one of the most powerful apotropaics known to demonology; conversely, because the mandrake is traditionally said to grow beneath gallows, it is an integral power of necromantic and black-magical incantations.

Manzanilla: Used as a hand wash for good luck in bingo and lotteries. Keep tickets with a packet of the herb.

Mistletoe: Apart from its holiday connection mistletoe has long been used to protect children from fairies, who cannot bring a changeling child into its presence. When burned it adds power

GYPSY WITCH PRESENTS:
TROPICAL SPELLS HOODOOS & VOODOOS

to exorcism rituals, and it is a useful protective herb when hung about a household.

Morning glory: Revered by the Aztecs and other Mesoamerican cultures for its powers to both prevent nightmares and induce visionary psychic states, morning glory, despite its toxicity, is widely used in infusions by the more courageous practitioners of herbal magick.

Mugwort: Popular tradition holds that John the Baptist wore a girdle of mugwort during his forty days in the wilderness, and since then, the herb has been invested with powerful qualities of divination, summoning, and prophecy. When burned with sandalwood or wormwood, it is an important component of scrying rituals, or it can be drunk as tea to heighten the power of divinatory rituals.

Mullein: Traditionally used as the wick in a sorcerer's or witch's oil lamp, mullein has a deep connection with both light and dark magick. In India, it is regarded as the most potent protective herb, and it can be substituted for graveyard dust in hoodoo charms. Various folk divinatory traditions employ mullein to prophesy love and good fortune, as well as to dispel demons.

Myrrh: Cited in the Bible as sacred, and used in purification rituals through the Middle East and Europe, myrrh enhances the power of any incense. The smoke is also used to consecrate holy tools and vessels.

Nettle: One of the nine sacred herbs of the Anglo-Saxons, nettles are used in various folk-magic traditions to capture a curse and send it back where it came from.

Oil of Abramelin: This oil is first mentioned in the demonology text The Sacred Magic of Abramelin the Mage. It is critical to the protection of the summoner in a demonic ritual and is composed of oil infused with cinnamon, myrrh, and galangal.

Orris Root: Cast a love spell by dusting it on the clothes of

GYPSY WITCH PRESENTS:
TROPICAL SPELLS HOODOOS & VOODOOS

the opposite sex and wear for attraction.

Palo Santo: Palo Santo or "Holy Wood" is a naturally perfumed resinous wood from a tree indigenous to Argentina and Paraguay. Palo Santo was known to the Incas as a spiritual remedy for purifying, cleansing, and ridding misfortune. It is used today as an aphrodisiac, ceremonial incense, and a natural insect repellent. To burn, light a stick, allow the wood to burn briefly - less than a minute, and then blow out the flame. Enjoy the fragrant lingering smoke which results. Each stick may be re-lit and used many times. Palo Santo can also be burned on charcoal, or slow simmered in water to release the natural resins.

Parsley: The Greeks associated parsley with death and kept it away from the table, believing it to have sprung from the blood of Archemorus, son of Eurydice, who was killed by a dragon when abandoned by his nurse. Thereafter parsley was considered a funereal plant and was dedicated to Persephone. The Romans, however, saw it as an emblem of good fortune.

Passion Flower: Brew into a tea and bathe in for 5 days to attract opposite sex.

Patchouli: Used in money and love rituals, incites lust, use in any ritual where graveyard dirt is required.

Poke Root: Breaks hexes by brewing it into a teas and adding it to bath water.

Quassia Chips: Mix with some hair of your beloved, burn and keep ashes in small bottle to preserve their love.

Queen of The Meadow: For good luck, make into a tea.

Queens Delight Root: Legends say that drinking a tea made from this root will help a woman conceive.

Queens Root: Take a bath in this when you wish to get married.

GYPSY WITCH PRESENTS:
TROPICAL SPELLS HOODOOS & VOODOOS

Rattle Snake Root: Put in a purple flannel bad for protection from sudden death and accident, keeps others from doing you wrong.

Rosemary: Versatile and useful in various magical contexts, rosemary promotes healing and purity. Used in charms and spells, it exerts a gentle binding influence. It can also be used to draw elves and fairies. Burned with charcoal, rosemary allows access to hidden knowledge.

Rue: Considered a powerful antimagickal herb since Hippocrates and other Greek physicians, rue is used as protection against hexes and is also incorporated into consecration rituals. It is also considered a defense against witchcraft and can give clairvoyance.

Sacred Bark: Keep in a bowl on your alter or reading table to help you concentrate.

Safflower: Mix with any jinx incense to cause destruction to an enemy, also used by gay men to bring on exciting sexual encounters by rubbing it on the inside of their knees.

Sage: An ambivalent but very useful herb, sage has long been associated with purification and fortune—both good and bad. Legendary for bringing prosperity and good fortune, sage must be cultivated carefully or its properties will reverse. Tradition holds that a homeowner must never plant sage in his own garden, and that unless sage is mixed in with other herbs, it will bring bad luck instead of good. Native American shamanic rituals began with the "smudging," or purification, of the ritual space by the burning of sage.

Scotch broom: Also known as broom top, this was a central part of druidic herbal magic. It can be boiled in salt water, and the combination of salt and the herb's own properties will ward off spirits and dispel poltergeists. Thrown into the air, it can raise winds; burned, it can calm them.

GYPSY WITCH PRESENTS: TROPICAL SPELLS HOODOOS & VOODOOS

Scullcap: To keep mate faithful, women should sew into his pillow some scullcap and two white lodestones in white flannel

Seaweed: Protection and summoning magic involving sailors, sea voyages, or ocean spirits often employed seaweed. In coastal areas, it is used to summon spirits and conduct séances with the ghosts of drowned sailors.

Solomon's Seal Root: Carry for protection and success, place on altar to ensure success with all rituals.

Southern John The Conqueror: Carry as a charm to bring luck in love and money matters.

Southernwood: Kept in the home as a love charm, burned to protect one from trouble.

Spanish moss: In areas where it grows natively, Spanish moss is an important part of rituals to banish poltergeists as well as to bring good fortune to a household. Often local traditions using Spanish moss also employ witch bottles to trap and disarm hostile enchantments.

Star anise: Used in purification rituals and to consecrate and protect holy sites in Buddhist and Shinto traditions, star anise also is known to Western traditions for its power to ward off the evil eye and protect against nightmares. Burned as incense, the seeds increase psychic awareness.

St. John's wort: A druidic sacred herb, St. John's wort repels demons and evil spirits, who cannot abide its smell. Carrying it provides protection against being beguiled by fairies and spirits.

Sumbul Root: A favorite love root, said to attract the opposite sex very quickly, carry on you or burn.

Thyme: Bathe in to ensure money at all times, add to jar and keep in home for good luck, use to cleanse magick areas and place in pillows to stop nightmares.

GYPSY WITCH PRESENTS: TROPICAL SPELLS HOODOOS & VOODOOS

Tobacco: Spirits from most Native American and Caribbean traditions enjoy offerings of tobacco, and the dried leaves were burned to open spirit channels as well as consecrate a ceremonial space.

Tonka Beans: A favorite hoodoo good luck charm that is used to make wishes come true.

Trumpet Weed: Used to make a man more potent, rubbed on member as a tea while hard.

Twitch Grass: Reverses hexes, causes trouble for enemies if thrown on their doorstep.

Unicorn Root: Carried for protection, used as a love charm, hide in loves belongings for love or hide two tied together to keep them faithful.

Van Van Oil: Van Van is an old hoodoo formula for oil, incense, sachet powders, and washing products that are designed to clear away evil, provide magickal protection, open the road to new prospects, change bad luck to good, and empower amulets and charms.

Vanillian: Powder can be burned with love incense to ensure that mate will always think of you.

Verbena: Bathe your children in this to help them learn faster. Burn with sandalwood for jinx removing.

Vervain: Also known as verbena, or "the witches' herb," vervain is powerful across a wide range of uses. It is considered a holy herb, bathe in for 7 days to bring money, used for love drawing and jinx removing.

Vetivert (Khus Khus): Placed in cash registers for increased business, burnt to overcome evil spells.

Violet: Used with other attraction herbs like lavender to bath in, helps those ill to heal faster.

GYPSY WITCH PRESENTS:
TROPICAL SPELLS HOODOOS & VOODOOS

Virginia Snake Root: Said to be best good luck charm but very expensive and hard to find.

Wahoo Bark: Also very hard to get, used to remove hexes.

Willow: The expression "knock on wood" comes from the practice of knocking on the willow tree to dispel evil, and the tree has an ancient association with rituals of protection, divination, and healing. The bark, burned with sandalwood, attracts spirits, especially if burned outdoors during a waning moon.

Witch Grass: Bathe in to attract a new lover, wear special witch perfume as well.

Woodruff: Good for victory, place in your left shoe before a game so your team will be victorious.

Yarrow: The flowers dispel negative influence and aid divination, while the twigs of the plant have been used in divination rituals throughout history. Yarrow stalks are the orthodox way to cast the I Ching and have been used in numerous other fortune-telling capacities as well. Also known as devil's nettle, yarrow can be used in summoning magick and divination involving commerce with demons.

Yucca: Native American rites used a hoop of twisted yucca fibers as a magical gateway. Jumping through the hoop would bring about transformation into animal form. A related magickal practice used a smaller ring of yucca, worn on the head, as a permanent talisman enabling the wearer to assume animal form.

GYPSY WITCH PRESENTS: TROPICAL SPELLS HOODOOS & VOODOOS

Black Snake Root Spell to Gain Money

This spell should be done during Waxing or Full Moon.

Soak Black Snake Root, also known as Black Cohosh and Squaw Root, in a cup of boiling water for fifteen minutes. The water is then strained and the root is thrown away. The liquid is put in a bottle and left for seven days.

On the eighth day, it is rubbed over the bottom of one's shoes so that the anointed will be led toward money; either to find it, win it, or gain it in some legal manner.

Vervain Protection Potion

To protect yourself and/or loved ones from all types of harm you will need to combine in a jar or bottle:

2/4's Cup of Spring Water
1 Teaspoon Vervain
2 Tablespoons Sea Salt
2 Tablespoons each of Frankincense and Myrrh

Sprinkle water very lightly around home in discreet places and anoint the bottom of your shoes and those of loved ones. Dispose of remainder immediately after use.

Binding Spell

This spell is for binding a violent or dangerous person from doing harm.

You will need a photo of person to be bound or a piece of white parchment paper with their whole name written on it in black ink or dove's blood ink. 18 inches or so of black silken cord or black thick string like embroidery floss. A small glass jar with cork lid, a small white candle and a small black candle.

GYPSY WITCH PRESENTS:
TROPICAL SPELLS HOODOOS & VOODOOS

Light both your candles and write the name on the paper or take the photograph in hand. Fold the paper or photo into as small a rectangle as possible.

Take the cord in hand and begin to wind it around the rectangle, for a total of nine loops, saying aloud in a clear, strong voice:

I (insert your name here), bind thee (insert name of offending person here) from causing harm to (insert name of victim here), from exerting control over this person, from influencing this person. I bind you from making further plans with this person.

I call upon the angels, Auriel, Michael, Gabriel, and Raphael to assist me in this righteous cause!

Place the paper into the jar. Urinate into the jar and cork. Seal all around the cork with the black candle wax.

Let the candles burn themselves out safely. Place this jar in a place where no one will disturb it.

House Protection Jar Spell

You will need: 1 glass jar, 1/2 to 1 cup salt, 3 cloves garlic, 9 bay leaves, 7 tsp. dried Basil, 4 tsp. dill seeds, 1tsp sage, 1tsp anise, 1tsp black pepper, 1tsp fennel, and 1 bowl.

In the morning, ideally on a bright sunny day, assemble the items.

Place in the bowl and say: *"Salt that protects, protect my home and all within."*

Add the cloves of garlic: *"Garlic that protects, protect my home and all within."*

Crumble the Bay leaves and place in the bowl: *"Bay that*

GYPSY WITCH PRESENTS:
TROPICAL SPELLS HOODOOS & VOODOOS

protects, protect my home and all within."

Add the basil and say: *"Basil that protects, protect my home and all within."*

Add the dill and say: *"Dill that protects, protect my home and all within."*

Add the sage and say: *"Sage that protects, protect my home and all within."*

Add the anise and say: *"Anise that protects, protect my home and all within."*

Add the fennel and say: *"Fennel that protects, protect my home and all within."*

Mix together the salt and the herbs with your hands, throughout the movement of your hands and fingers lend energy to the potent protective items, visualize your home safe and as a shining secure place. Pour the mixture in the jar and cap tightly,

Place it in your home with these words: *"Salt and herbs, nine times nine Guard now this home of mine"*

Fertility Spell

You will need: 1 watermelon, 1 tbs. powdered Palo Dulce, 1 cup mixed rice and beans, 1 tbs. shredded coconut, 2 tbs. fresh basil leaves, 1 tbs. anil powder, 1 tbs. river water, 1 tbs. sea water, 2 cups molasses, 3 cups olive oil, 7 pennies, 1 wick Statue of Yemaya.

Cut the watermelon in half and scoop the majority of the insides out. Write you name 7 times on a brown piece of paper. Place the paper at the bottom of the watermelon.

Place the 7 pennies on the paper. Place the powdered Palo

GYPSY WITCH PRESENTS:
TROPICAL SPELLS HOODOOS & VOODOOS

Dulce, rice, and beans, shredded coconut and fresh basil leaves in the watermelon. Pour the river water and the sea water into the watermelon. Pour the molasses into the watermelon. Pour the olive oil into the watermelon.

Mix the anil into the olive oil and float the wick on top of the oil. Light the wick and allow it to burn for 7 days.

Place the watermelon lamp next to the stature of Yemaya. On the 8th day, bring the watermelon and leave it next to a body of water.

You may also want to make a lotion by placing 1 cup of unscented body lotion or body cream in a mixing bowl. Mix in the following ingredients: 10 drops coconut oil, 10 drops chrysanthemum oil, 20 drops watermelon oil.

Anoint yourself with the lotion for as long as you are trying to conceive.

The Lemon Curse Spell

Items needed: 1 lemon, 1 black candle, 9 nails, Cursing Oil, Picture of person (to be cursed), Athame Black bowl.

Light the candle. Cut a slit into the lemon and place the picture of the person inside the slit. Take one if the nails and feel your anger rise and pierce the nail into the lemon. Do the same for the remaining nails.

With each nail your anger should rise for this person getting blacker and blacker. When you reach the last nail, place the lemon in the bowl.

Pour cursing oil onto the lemon filling the bowl until the lemon is half covered (with oil.) Let the lemon rot in this bowl, and as the lemon rots, so too will the life and luck of the person.

GYPSY WITCH PRESENTS:
TROPICAL SPELLS HOODOOS & VOODOOS

Spell to Cause a Distant Love to Think of You

You will need: dried rue, rosemary or tansy, a running stream (river, lake, ocean).

Cast dried herbs of rue, rosemary, (or tansy) into a running stream while calling out to him/her.

As the herbs are carried away, visualize them carrying your message of love to your beloved.

Love Potion

You will need a few large apples, cinnamon, yarrow, spring water, salt, and an enameled or cast-iron saucepan.

Concentrate on your goal while preparing this potion: Slice the apples place them into the saucepan, coat with cinnamon, and cover with yarrow.

Put in enough water to submerge the contents and add a small sprinkling of salt. Stir clockwise on low heat, incanting a love charm of your own making. Bring to a simmer for about 90 minutes, strain and place into a dark jar.

Put a few drops into your favorite aftershave or cologne and wear it every 4 days. The spell continues to work even after the scent fades.

Vervain Spell to Rid Yourself of an Unwanted Lover

Some people are wooed by persistent would-be lovers, those who won't take no for an answer and who won't leave them alone. This is the ideal spell for such a situation. It should be done during the waning cycle of the Moon.

Have a roaring fire going, then go outside and pick up two handfuls of dry vervain leaves (you can place them on the

GYPSY WITCH PRESENTS:
TROPICAL SPELLS HOODOOS & VOODOOS

ground ahead of time, if necessary).

As you pick them up, shout out the name of the one you wish to be rid of.

Turn and go into the house (or cross to the fire if this is all done out in the open) and fling leaves onto the fire with the words:

> *Here is my pain;*
> *Take it and soar.*
> *Depart from me now*
> *And offend me no more.*

Do this for three nights in a row and you will hear no more from the unwanted ones.

Luck and Wishes Charm

You will need a Tiger's eye (gemstone), nutmeg, allspice, and a charm (e.g. rabbits foot).

Hold the tiger's eye in one hand and the charm in your other hand. Meditate for a few moments, see yourself and see what your luck could bring.

Now sprinkle the nutmeg and the allspice on the charm.

Say these words, filling the blanks with what your charm is:

> "_____, _____ *bring me good luck.*
> *May my luck change from this day forward.*
> _____, _____ *bring me good luck.*"

Be sure to keep your charm on you at all times. If your luck doesn't change after a few weeks, recharge the charm again with this spell.

GYPSY WITCH PRESENTS: TROPICAL SPELLS HOODOOS & VOODOOS

Corn Wealth Spell

For wealth and prosperity for a year, take the husk from an ear of corn and put a dollar bill along with a note written on parchment:

Oh, dear god of luck,
money is like muck,
not good except it be spread.
Spread some here at--------------(write in your address).
Thanks be to thee. Amen.

Sign your name.

Sprinkle the dollar bill and note with Coltsfoot leaves. Roll the husk up and tie together with green string or ribbon.

Hang the token up above the entryway with green cord. That husk should bring riches into your home or business by the bushel.

Money Spell with Smartweed

To find money, one should make a conjure bag containing a magnetic horseshoe, and a lodestone to attract and draw wealth to you. You will also need some Smartweed to enable you to see how to capture it and hold it without being led astray by unprofitable distractions or foolish delays.

Feed your money bag with a sprinkle of Gold Magnetic Sand every third day until you find the amount you need.

Lavender Money Spell

A lucky money spell is made by placing in a conjure bag seven pieces of money, each different, such as a penny, nickel, dime, quarter, a half dollar, $1.00 bill, and $5.00 bill, all of which are sprinkled liberally with lavender.

GYPSY WITCH PRESENTS:
TROPICAL SPELLS HOODOOS & VOODOOS

Take the bag with you for seven days and your money should multiply seven times (this would give you $41.46 above your original investment) or, in some instances, seven times seven. This would result in a tidy sum of $338.50.

Luck Hand Rood Money Spell

To get and hold a job, always carry a Lucky Hand Root on your person. Use Lucky Nine Oil on your wrists each day for nine days, and burn some John the Conqueror Incense each night. These roots bring luck in all undertakings and no conjure bag would be considered complete without one.

The hands are usually imperfect, but this does not affect their value as a talisman. The ones which are formed so that all five fingers are distinguishable are very rare.

**GYPSY WITCH PRESENTS:
TROPICAL SPELLS HOODOOS & VOODOOS**

If you enjoyed this book, write for our free catalog:

Global Communications
P.O. Box 753
New Brunswick, NJ   08903

www.conspiracyjournal.com

www.ingramcontent.com/pod-product-compliance
Lightning Source LLC
Chambersburg PA
CBHW081233170426
43198CB00017B/2748